global

PRE-INTERMEDIATE
workbook
with key

Julie Moore

with additional material by Rob Metcalf

Contents

UNIT 1	Individual & Society	3
UNIT 2	Eating & Drinking	10
UNIT 3	Art & Music	18
UNIT 4	Hopes & Fears	25
UNIT 5	Work & Leisure	33
UNIT 6	Science & Technology	41
UNIT 7	Time & Money	50
UNIT 8	Home & Away	58
UNIT 9	Health & Fitness	65
UNIT 10	New & Old	72

| Audioscript | 82 |
| Answer Key | 86 |

UNIT 1 Individual & Society

Grammar 1A
Word order in questions

Complete the sentences with the correct word.

1. Where *do / does / are* you work?
2. What *do / does / is* the company do?
3. Where *does / is / are* your office?
4. *Do / Are / Does* you drive to work?
5. *Do / Is / Are* you a full-time employee?
6. When *did / was / were* you start your current job?
7. What qualifications *does / are / do* you have?
8. *Does / Do / Are* you enjoy your job?

Grammar 1B
Word order in questions

Complete the questions with the correct auxiliary verb *do* or *be*.

1. Q: _____ you married?
   A: Yes, my husband's name is Isaac.
2. Q: _____ you have any children?
   A: Yes, I have two sons.
3. Q: What _____ their names?
   A: Jacob and Daniel.
4. Q: Where _____ you work?
   A: I'm a nurse at the local hospital.
5. Q: _____ you enjoy your job?
   A: Yes, I love helping people.
6. Q: What _____ your husband do?
   A: He works in a bank.
7. Q: When _____ you meet him?
   A: We were at university together.

Grammar 2
what and *how* questions

Complete the questions with *how* or *what*.

1. a _____ kind of car do you drive?
   b It's just an ordinary little car.
2. a _____ many doors does it have?
   b It's a four-door, so it's easy to get in the back.
3. a _____ colour is it?
   b It's silver.
4. a _____ old is it?
   b It's about 4 years old now.
5. a _____ size engine does it have?
   b It's a 1.4 litre, so it goes quite well.
6. a _____ fast does it go?
   b I mostly drive in town, so I don't go very fast.
7. a _____ reliable is it?
   b It's very good. It never breaks down.

Grammar 3
Present simple

Complete the text about junk mail using the correct form of the verbs in brackets.

We all (1) _____ (*hate*) junk mail, but how can we stop it? Businesses (2) _____ (*send*) millions of emails every year and most people just (3) _____ (*put*) them straight in the recycling bin. But how (4) _____ (*do*) companies (5) _____ (*get*) your name and address in the first place? Every time you (6) _____ (*give*) your details to a company, for example, when you (7) _____ (*order*) something, the company (8) _____ (*add*) your name to their mailing list. But what's worse, that company often (9) _____ (*sell*) that list to other companies and so their customers' personal details (10) _____ (*be*) soon on many more mailing lists. As a result, the unlucky customer then (11) _____ (*have*) even more junk mail that he (12) _____ (*not want*).

Grammar 4
Frequency adverbs

Complete the sentences by putting the frequency adverbs and expressions in the correct place.

1. I take my keys with me when I go out. (always)
   _____
   _____

2. I carry my wallet with me. (usually)
   _____
   _____

3. I pay for things by credit card, but I have some cash in my wallet for small things. (often, always)
   _____
   _____

4. My mobile phone is in my pocket. (almost always)
   _____
   _____

Unit 1 Individual & Society

5 I go to the gym so my bag is full of my sports clothes. (every morning, usually)
_____
_____

6 I take a bag with me; I just put things in my pockets. (hardly ever, usually)
_____
_____

Grammar 5
Present continuous

Are the sentences correct or incorrect? Circle your answer.

1 Scientists are studying world temperatures.
Correct / Incorrect

2 Weather around the world is changing.
Correct / Incorrect

3 Politicians aren't agreeing about climate change.
Correct / Incorrect

4 Global energy use is increasing every year.
Correct / Incorrect

5 Car companies are now developing electric cars.
Correct / Incorrect

6 Many people are still preferring to drive rather than walk.
Correct / Incorrect

7 People are often forgetting to switch off lights.
Correct / Incorrect

8 We are all needing to change our lifestyles.
Correct / Incorrect

Vocabulary 1A
Describing people

Write the words in the box under the correct heading below.

| bald   curly   fat   medium-height |
| middle-aged   old   overweight   short |
| slim   straight   tall   young |

Hair	Height	Weight	Age

Vocabulary 1B
Describing people

a   b   c   d

Match the descriptions to the pictures.

1 He's bald.
Picture _____

2 He's got short, brown hair.
Picture _____

3 He's in his early twenties.
Picture _____

4 He's in his late forties.
Picture _____

5 She's an older woman.
Picture _____

6 She's got blond, curly hair.
Picture _____

7 She's got shoulder-length, red hair.
Picture _____

8 She's in her twenties.
Picture _____

Extend your vocabulary 1
look and *look like*

Complete the sentences with *look*, *looks*, *look like* or *looks like*.

1 That's my new boss. I think she _____ a film star.

2 Yes, she _____ very attractive. She _____ a fashion model to me.

3 And she _____ very young. She doesn't _____ a manager.

4 Our boss doesn't _____ her. He's an old guy.

5 He's only about 50, but he _____ much older.

6 He's got grey hair and a beard. He _____ my grandfather!

Individual & Society

Vocabulary 2A
People you know

Write the words in the box under the correct heading below.

| acquaintance brother classmate |
| colleague husband neighbour |
| sister wife |

Friends	Family

Vocabulary 2B
People you know

Complete the words to describe the people in the sentences below.

1 I saw Rhonna this afternoon. You know I go to a yoga class? Well, she's one of my c_____.
2 Isn't that Damien's w_____? I haven't seen her since their wedding.
3 I don't know much about Damien's family. He's only an a_____.
4 I'll ask Nadja to translate it. She's a c_____ of mine from work.
5 I got an email from Anna today. She's an old f_____ from university.
6 If I'm not at home, you can leave the parcel with my n_____, Mrs Park.

Extend your vocabulary 2
in touch

Complete the text with the words in the box.

| get in keep lost out of with |

I'm not (1) _____ touch with most of my school friends now. I (2) _____ touch with a lot of people when I went to university. I do stay in touch (3) _____ one or two good friends though. We meet up whenever we can.

A lot of my friends from university live abroad, but we (4) _____ in touch via email. And I recently found some old friends through a social networking site. We'd been (5) _____ touch for a while, so it's interesting to (6) _____ back in touch with them and to hear about their lives now.

Extend your vocabulary 3
Expressions with *place*

Choose the correct words to complete the text.

A fun run (1) *takes place / takes part* in our town every year to raise money for charity. I always go to watch, but I'm not really a runner, so I've never (2) *taken place / taken part*. Last year, one of my colleagues was planning to run. But she hurt her foot the week before and she asked me to run (3) *in place of her / for her place*. For some reason, I agreed. After all, it was for charity.

When I arrived on the morning of the run, there were really fit people (4) *in all the place / all over the place*. They were all wearing proper running clothes and doing stretching exercises. I felt completely (5) *out of place / wrong place*! I almost went straight home. Why did I agree (6) *in the first place / at first part*? But it was too late to change my mind. My colleague had collected lots of money for charity and it wasn't (7) *at my place / my place* to disappoint everyone. I did finish the race, but I'm never going to agree to something like that again!

Unit 1 Individual & Society

Pronunciation 1
The alphabet

🔊 **1.01** Listen and complete the details below.

1 Name: Dr. Claudia _____
2 Email: _____@globalnet.com
3 Address: 35 _____ Street, Athens
4 Employer: _____ Consulting
5 Place of birth: _____, Scotland
6 Location: _____ Park

Pronunciation 2
Word linking

🔊 **1.02** Listen and choose the sentence you hear.

1 a What do you do here?
  b What are you doing there?
  c What to do here?
2 a I take care to computer system.
  b I take care of the computer system.
  c I'm to care for your computer system.
3 a So I can ask you for help with IT problems.
  b So I can ask you to help my IT problems.
  c So I ask you to help to IT problems.
4 a No, you have call to help desk to that.
  b No, you are to call a help desk first.
  c No, you have to call the help desk for that.
5 a No, what a number?
  b Oh, what's the number?
  c Oh, where is the number?

Listening
Identical twins

🔊 **1.03** Listen to Alison talking about her twin sister and answer the questions.

1 What did the sisters look like when they were young?
  a Quite similar.
  b Exactly the same.
2 How old are they now?
  a They're about 30–34 years old.
  b They're about 36–39 years old.
3 Why is Alison slimmer than her sister?
  a Because she eats less.
  b Because she does more exercise.
4 What does Alison look like?
  a She's quite slim, with short hair.
  b She's tall, with long, brown hair.
5 What does her sister usually wear?
  a She wears skirts or dresses.
  b She wears trousers or shorts.
6 What is the sisters' relationship like now?
  a They don't see each other much.
  b They're close.

1 Individual & Society

Reading
A mobile global population

1 Before you read, answer these questions.
1 Do you live in the same town or village as your parents and grandparents?
2 Why do people move from one place to another?

2 Read the first part of the article *A mobile global population* and answer the questions.
1 Give three reasons why people move.
2 When a family moves, how does it affect parents, children and grandparents?

3 Read the second part of the article. Are these statements true or false?
1 In many countries, people are moving from villages to cities.
2 People mostly move to the city for education.
3 Children live with their parents in the city.

4 Find words or expressions in the text with these meanings.
1 people in a family of about the same age
2 all the people who live in an area or a country
3 the process of cities getting bigger
4 people living in the countryside

5 Complete the text using the correct form of the verbs in brackets.

In 1950, only New York City had a population of more than 10 million. Now more than 20 cities around the world (1) _____ (*have*) more than 10 million residents and many cities (2) _____ (*get*) bigger. Tokyo, in Japan, (3) _____ (*be*) the largest city in the world with a population of more than 34 million. Almost 22 million people (4) _____ (*live*) in the city of Jakarta in the Philippines. New York City and Seoul both (5) _____ (*have*) populations of around 20 million. Seven cities in the top ten (6) _____ (*be*) in Asia. Europe (7) _____ (*not have*) a city in the top ten. Cities in Africa and Asia (8) _____ (*grow*) the most quickly.

A mobile global population

In the past, most people lived in the same place for their whole life. You stayed in the village where you were born. So, several generations of the same family – children, parents, grandparents – all lived in the same area, the same street or even the same house. It wasn't common for people to move away from their home town.

1 A mobile workforce
Nowadays, we have a highly mobile global population. People are moving around all the time; for work, for education or for a better life. But what problems does this cause for society? People lose touch with old friends and colleagues, and they are always trying to build new social networks. A new job in a new city often means a move for the whole family. How does this affect family relationships? Children have to change schools and get to know new teachers and classmates. Grandparents often live many kilometres away from their grandchildren. Better communications mean that we can stay in touch by telephone or email, but you can't email Grandma's apple pie or play with Grandpa via text.

2 Urbanisation
In many countries with fast-growing economies, like China and India, thousands of people are moving to cities from the countryside. Cities in Asia are some of the fastest-growing in the world. People don't want to work on the family farm when there are more job opportunities in the city. It is common for parents to leave their village to find work in the city. The result? Many villages are now full of only children and old people. What is the future for these rural communities?

Individual & Society

Writing
Writing about people

Reading and note-taking

1 Read the profile from a university website.

Staff Profile

Name: Dr Rosalind Newton

Position: English lecturer

Rosalind teaches English to overseas students in the School of Languages. Her colleagues and students call her Ros.

Ros was born in Australia and she studied English and Education in the United States. Then she taught English at universities in Brazil and Japan. She speaks several foreign languages and she still enjoys travelling around the world.

She teaches on several courses for overseas students at the university, including General English and English for Academic Purposes. As well as teaching, she writes books for English students.

In her spare time, she loves walking in the countryside with her husband, Alan and their dog, Zuma.

---

2 Use the text to make notes about the type of information included in a personal profile. For example, full name.

_____
_____
_____
_____
_____
_____
_____

Language focus: linking ideas together

3 Read the profile from the website of a design company. Join the ideas together using words in the box.

| also | and | both | but | so | too |

Willdesign

About us

Niki and Rob Willis work in a studio next to their house in the small village of Sawston, near Cambridge. They (1) _____ studied Design at the London School of Art (2) _____ they started their own design company, called Willdesign, in 2003.

They mostly design book covers for large publishing companies, (3) _____ they sometimes make leaflets for local businesses (4) _____. They love reading (5) _____ they try to design covers which will catch the imagination of readers. Rob (6) _____ creates websites.

Preparing to write

4 You are helping to write a website for your school, college or company. Make notes about a classmate or colleague. Use the topics below and your own ideas.

Name:

Job title/subject:

Work/studies:

Interests/free time:

Unit 1 Individual & Society

Writing

5 Use your notes to write a profile of your classmate or colleague. Include some personal information and some information about their studies or work.

Writing skills: checking your work for errors

6 Read what you have written and think about the following questions.

- Is there any information which is not appropriate for a website?
- Is there any other important or interesting information you can add?
- Have you joined your ideas together, for example using *and*, *but* or *so*?

7 Now check your writing for errors. Below is a list of possible problem areas.

- spelling
- punctuation
- remember capital letters for names – *Sarah* (not ~~*sarah*~~)
- verb forms – e.g. *he + has* (not ~~*he have*~~)
- verb tenses – present, past, etc.
- articles – *a*, *an*, *the*, etc.

Not sure about a spelling? Don't just guess - check in a dictionary!

Make any changes before you give your writing to your teacher.

UNIT 2 Eating & Drinking

Grammar 1A
Countable and uncountable nouns

Write the words in the box under the correct heading below.

| bread | chocolate | coffee | meat | ~~nut~~ | ~~pasta~~ |
| potato | sandwich | soup | steak | | |

countable	countable or uncountable	uncountable
nut		pasta

Grammar 1B
Countable and uncountable nouns

Choose the correct quantifiers to complete the conversation.

A: I've cooked (1) *a / an* casserole for us.
B: That looks nice. What's it made of?
A: There's (2) *any / some* meat, I've used lamb. Then there are (3) *– / an* onions, carrots and mushrooms. I've also cooked (4) *a / some* potatoes to go with it.
B: Mmm, it smells great.
A: What would you like to drink? I've got (5) *some / any* red wine or perhaps (6) *a / some* glass of water?
B: Have you got (7) *a / any* mineral water?
A: Yes, I think there's (8) *a / –* bottle of (9) *– / some* sparkling mineral water in the fridge.

Grammar 2A
Quantifiers

Choose *much* or *many* to complete the questions.

1 How *much / many* oil do I need for the casserole?
2 How *much / many* different ingredients are there?
3 How *much / many* onions does it say?
4 How *much / many* carrots do I need to cut?
5 How *much / many* cheese is there in the fridge?
6 How *much / many* minutes does it need to cook?
7 How *much / many* salt shall I add?
8 How *much / many* people does the casserole serve?

Grammar 2B
Quantifiers

Complete the sentences with the quantifiers in the box.

| a few | a little | a lot of | enough |
| many | much | too many | |

1 'Boil fresh vegetables for just _____ minutes.'
2 'Make sure you drink _____ water, especially in hot weather.'
3 '_____ people eat junk food instead of cooking with fresh ingredients. But do you know how _____ salt and sugar there is in what you eat?'
4 'It's OK to have _____ sugar in your diet, but you shouldn't eat _____ sweet things.'
5 'How _____ cups of coffee do you drink each day?'

Grammar 3
The infinitive

Complete the sentences using the correct form of the verbs in brackets. Use *to* where needed.

1 If you want _____ (cook) Chinese food, it's important _____ (have) a good saucepan.
2 Most Chinese dishes are quick and easy _____ (make).
3 I try _____ (use) fresh ingredients, so I _____ (go) to the market every day.
4 Sometimes it's difficult _____ (find) Chinese ingredients.
5 Most European supermarkets don't _____ (sell) things like chicken's feet.
6 You need _____ (visit) special Asian shops, then you can usually _____ (get) what you need.

Eating & Drinking

Grammar 4
The infinitive of purpose

Write to in the correct place in each of the seven instructions.

1 Before you start cooking, check the recipe make sure you have all the ingredients.
2 You will need an onion, some garlic, some beef and a tin of tomatoes make a basic pasta sauce.
3 Put some oil in a frying pan cook while you cut the onions and garlic.
4 Fry the onions and garlic gently. Be careful, it's easy burn them.
5 Add the meat to the pan. Keep stirring everything stop it from sticking.
6 Pour in the tomatoes and stir well mix.
7 Cover the pan and leave it cook gently for 45 minutes.

Vocabulary 1A
Food

Match the foods 1–4 with the tastes a–d.

1 sea water   a bitter
2 Indian curry   b sweet
3 honey   c salty
4 fresh lemon juice   d spicy

Vocabulary 1B
Food

Complete the food words.

1 I usually have something sweet for b_____, perhaps some yoghurt with honey.
2 Most days I have a sandwich for my l_____.
3 If I'm really busy, I e_____ my sandwich at my desk.
4 During the afternoon, I often have a s_____, maybe some fruit.
5 I love spicy food, so we often have an Indian curry for d_____.
6 I cook a meat or a vegetable curry and I s_____ it with rice.

Extend your vocabulary
taste

Complete the sentences with the phrases in the box.

| bitter taste | tastes awful | taste like |
| tastes of | taste sweet | |

1 The crackers are so dry, they _____ cardboard.
2 This milk _____, I think it's gone bad.
3 The berries _____ and the birds love to eat them.
4 Coffee sometimes has a slightly _____.
5 I tried some Dutch soda that _____ bananas!

Vocabulary 2A
In the kitchen

Match the words in the box with the pictures.

| fork | frying pan | knife | plate | saucepan | spoon |

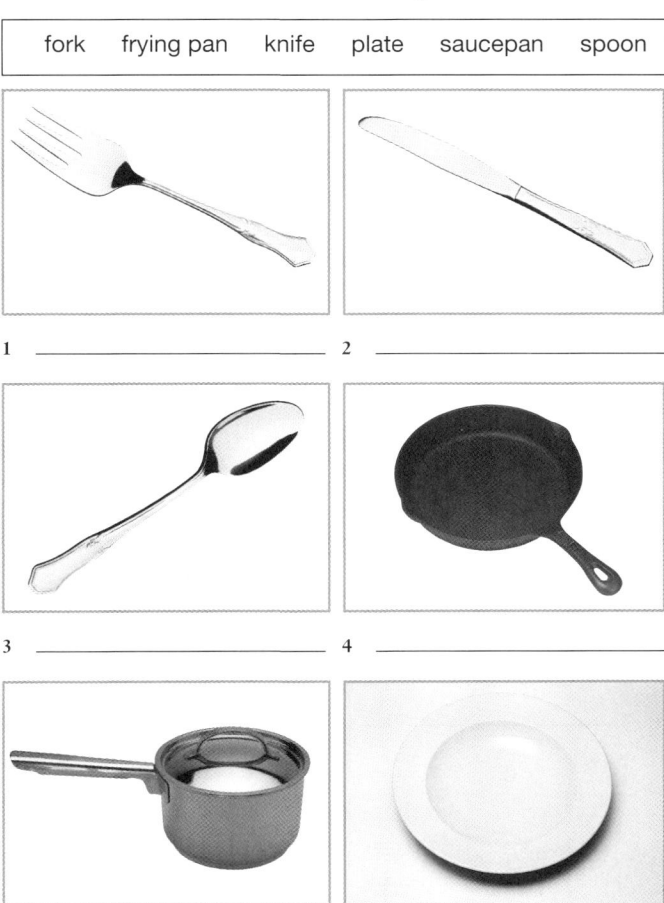

1 _____   2 _____
3 _____   4 _____
5 _____   6 _____

Unit 2

UNIT 2 Eating & Drinking

Vocabulary 2B
In the kitchen

Match the kitchen items 1–6 with their uses a–f.

1 saucepan   a to cut the vegetables
2 bowls   b to serve the steak on
3 spoons   c to cook the soup
4 knife   d to cook the steak
5 frying pan   e to serve the soup in
6 plates   f to eat the soup with

Vocabulary 3A
Containers and drinks

Complete the descriptions under the pictures.

1 a _____ of coffee   2 a _____ of wine

3 a _____ of water   4 a _____ of orange juice

5 a _____ of tea

Vocabulary 3B
Containers and drinks

Choose the correct words to complete the sentences.

1 Can I have *two coffees / two coffee*, please?
2 Would you like *some milk / a milk* in your coffee?
3 I usually drink *a tea / tea* without *any milk / some milk*.
4 Is there *any orange juice / a bottle orange juice* in the fridge?
5 They celebrated with *a few glasses / some glass* of champagne.
6 Is it safe to drink *tap's water / the tap water* here?

Vocabulary 4
The human body

Complete the puzzle.

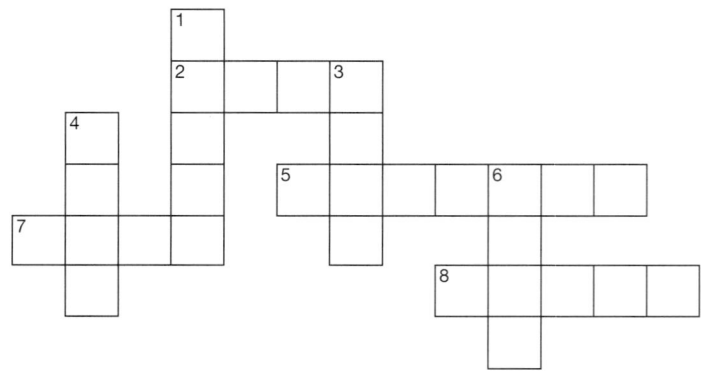

Across

2 You use these to see with. (4)
5 You have ten of these. (7)
7 You put shoes on these. (4)
8 You use this to think. (5)

Down

1 This works faster when you exercise. (5)
3 This covers your whole body. (4)
4 Where your leg bends in the middle. (4)
6 You use these to hear with. (4)

UNIT 2 Eating & Drinking

Pronunciation 1
/k/ and /tʃ/

🔊 **1.04** Listen and put the words in the box in the correct columns.

brea**k**fast	**c**ake	**c**arton	**ch**eese
sna**ck**	**ch**ewing gum	**ch**op	**c**up
ice **c**ubes	ma**tch**		

/k/	/tʃ/

Pronunciation 2
to and *too*

🔊 **1.05** Listen to the sentences and tick (✔) the correct pronunciation of the underlined word.

		/tə/	/tuː/
1	There's <u>too</u> much salt in the sauce.		
2	It's important <u>to</u> cook meat properly.		
3	You need <u>to</u> add some more sugar.		
4	Put the wine in the fridge <u>to</u> chill.		
5	Try <u>to</u> eat plenty of fruit and vegetables.		
6	I'll have a cup of coffee and a glass of water <u>too</u>, please.		
7	I offered <u>to</u> make him a cup of coffee.		

Listening
Clean drinking water

🔊 **1.06** Listen to someone talking about a special drinking straw. Are the statements true or false?

1 Many people around the world don't have clean drinking water. _____
2 Dirty water causes disease. _____
3 There are no water purification facilities in poor countries. _____
4 The straw contains special chemicals. _____
5 The straws are very simple to use. _____
6 These straws are the best way to provide clean water for everyone. _____

Unit 2 Eating & Drinking

Reading
The world's best diets

1 What do you know about the food people eat in Europe and North America? Choose the correct words to complete the sentences.

1 People eat *a little / a lot of* fast food.
2 People eat *a little / a lot of* processed food.
3 People *eat / don't eat* enough fruit and vegetables.

2 Read the first part of the article *The world's best diets* and check your answers.

3 Read the rest of the article and match the comments with one or more of these diets : the Mediterranean (M), the Japanese (J), the Latin American (LA) or the French (F).

1 'We eat a lot of fish.'
   _____
2 'We never eat too much food.'
   _____
3 'Nuts are an important part of our diet.'
   _____
4 'We only eat a little meat.'
   _____
5 'We eat some unhealthy things.'
   _____
6 'It's important not to eat too fast.'
   _____

4 Answer the questions.
1 What do you need if you want to change your eating habits?
   _____
   _____
   _____

2 In Western countries, why isn't information about eating habits clear?
   _____
   _____
   _____

3 How many people in Mediterranean countries follow a Mediterranean diet?
   _____
   _____
   _____

4 What two things are special about Japanese food?
   _____
   _____
   _____

5 Why is France an exception?
   _____
   _____
   _____

6 What does the French diet tell us about healthy eating?
   _____
   _____
   _____

5 Complete the second sentence so that it has the same meaning as the first sentence. Write one word on each line.

1 In Western countries, some people don't have any time for cooking.
   In Western countries, some people have _____ _____ for cooking.

2 People often eat more food than they need.
   People often eat _____ _____ food.

3 Not many people eat enough fruit and vegetables.
   Only _____ _____ people eat enough fruit and vegetables.

4 You can help children eat fruit if you make a fruit drink with it.
   _____ _____ children eat fruit, make a fruit drink with it.

5 Knowing what food is bad for you can be difficult.
   It can be difficult _____ _____ what food is bad for you.

6 We have some information about healthy eating, but we need more.
   We _____ have _____ information about healthy eating.

Unit 2

Eating & Drinking

The world's best diets

For many people in Western countries, food is a difficult topic. They know their Western diet, with a lot of processed and fast food, contains too much salt, sugar and fat. But to change eating habits takes time and clear information, and both can be difficult to find, especially when experts change their advice about what food is good and bad for you.

Unfortunately, the Western diet is becoming popular in other parts of the world too. To stop a global health problem, we need to learn from places where people still have healthy eating habits.

One example is the countries around the Mediterranean Sea in Europe. The traditional diet of this area is one of the world's healthiest. People eat a lot of vegetables, beans, nuts and fruit, quite a lot of fish, some chicken, and not much meat. Unfortunately, many people in this region have lost their traditional food habits.

Japan is another place with good eating habits. It's one of the countries in the world where people live the longest, healthiest lives. People there eat a lot of fish, vegetables and fruit. Also, Japanese food *looks* good, and portions are small. People eat slowly, they eat less and really *taste* their food.

The traditional diet of many Latin American countries is also very healthy. All meals include vegetables, beans, nuts and fruit. What's more, people eat fish or chicken every day, and don't eat much meat.

However, there are exceptions to the rule. Many people in France live long, healthy lives, but they eat some things that are not healthy. But in France food is important. People enjoy eating together and they don't eat too much. Perhaps a healthy diet is not just about ingredients, it's also about *how* people eat.

Unit 2 Eating & Drinking

Writing
Describing food and drink
Reading & Vocabulary

1 Read the descriptions of two restaurants.

River Bistro

The River Bistro serves simple, healthy, delicious food. We use fresh local ingredients and our menu changes daily. For lunch, we serve a selection of tasty soups and fresh sandwiches. Why not visit in the afternoon for tea or coffee and a piece of cake? We have a selection of cakes, including our delicious chocolate cake. In the evening, you can choose from our menu of fish, meat and vegetarian dishes. All our dishes come with fresh vegetables.

Hot Wok

Our menu offers typical dishes from Japan, Thailand, Malaysia and Indonesia. We use original Asian recipes to create an exciting balance of tastes. Our menu includes curries, noodles and rice dishes. Why not try our Singapore noodles with fish, chicken and fresh vegetables, all cooked with a special mixture of spices? You can watch your food being prepared and cooked in our open kitchen. When you place your order, our experienced Asian chefs cook your dish immediately from fresh ingredients. This is fresh, healthy, tasty fast food!

2 Use the texts to make notes about vocabulary used to describe food.

food adjectives	food nouns

3 What type of food do you like to eat in restaurants? Think of your favourite restaurant and add any words to the lists above to describe the food.

Writing skills: making your writing more interesting

4 Add some adjectives to the descriptions below to make them more interesting.

1 They serve a range of salads made from vegetables.

_____

2 My favourite dish consists of chicken, noodles and sauce.

_____

3 The restaurant's speciality is cake.

_____

4 All the dishes are made from ingredients.

_____

5 For lunch, there's a choice of sandwiches and soup.

_____

Eating & Drinking

Preparing to write

5 Make notes about your favourite restaurant. Think about the dishes they serve and the style and taste of the food.

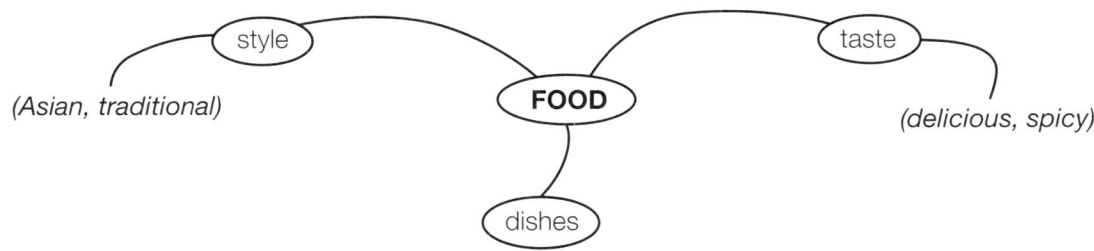

Writing

Write a description of your favourite restaurant. Describe the style of food and some dishes. Use adjectives to make the restaurant sound interesting.

Useful language

- They serve …
- They use … ingredients …
- The menu includes …
- You can choose from …
- dishes come with/are served with …
- a selection of wines/cakes/vegetables

UNIT 2 Art & Music

Grammar 1A
Regular past tense forms

Complete these sentences with the past simple forms of the verbs in brackets.

1. I _____ (watch) a great film at the weekend.
2. The band _____ (play) for almost two hours.
3. He _____ (study) Art at college.
4. In the afternoon, we _____ (visit) an art gallery.
5. A museum worker _____ (drop) the vase and it _____ (smash) on the floor.
6. She _____ (press) a button and the music _____ (stop).
7. We _____ (plan) to go to the concert, but we _____ (arrive) too late.

Grammar 1B
Irregular past tense forms

Complete the sentences with the correct form of the irregular verbs.

1. In 1987, Yasuo Goto *paid / payed* almost $40 million dollars for Van Gogh's *Sunflowers*.
2. JK Rowling *wrote / written* the first Harry Potter book using an old-fashioned typewriter.
3. The family of painter Paul Gaugin *left /leaved* France in 1851 and *gone / went* to Peru.
4. Mark Chapman *shooted / shot* musician John Lennon outside his New York apartment in 1980.
5. Writer Gabriel García Márquez *won / wind* the Nobel Prize for Literature in 1982.
6. In 2004, thieves *stealt / stole* the painting *The Scream* from the Munch Museum in Oslo.
7. Norwegian police *found / founded* the missing painting two years later.

Grammar 2
Past simple and past continuous

Complete the texts with the past simple or past continuous forms of the verbs in brackets.

Nick Hornby (1) _____ (begin) writing while he (2) _____ (study) English Literature at Cambridge University. After he (3) _____ (finish) university, he (4) _____ (have) several different jobs. Among other things, he (5) _____ (teach) English to foreign students. He (6) _____ (work) as a journalist when he (7) _____ (write) his first book, *High Fidelity*, in 1995.

Author JK Rowling also (8) _____ (work) as an English teacher in Portugal. Apparently, the idea for the Harry Potter books (9) _____ (come) to her while she (10) _____ (sit) on a train to London. She (11) _____ (complete) the first novel in 1995 while she (12) _____ (live) in Edinburgh.

Grammar 3A
Used to

Complete the sentences with the correct form of the verb.

1. As a teenager, I *used listen / used to listen* to really loud rock music.
2. I *didn't use to like / didn't used to like* classical music at all.
3. I *used to go / used to went* to the local record shop every weekend.
4. Music *was used to / used to be* on vinyl records then, not CDs.
5. My parents *used to complaining / used to complain* that I played my records too loud.
6. What music *did you use to like / used you to like* as a teenager?

Art & Music

Grammar 3B
Used to

Rewrite these sentences with *used to*.

1 Before television, people *listened* to the radio for news.
   _____
   _____

2 People *went* to the cinema to watch news films.
   _____
   _____

3 In the early days of TV, there *weren't* programmes all day.
   _____
   _____

4 Families *sat* together around the TV in the evening.
   _____
   _____

5 When I was young, we *had* a black and white TV.
   _____
   _____

6 And there *weren't* as many different TV channels as there are today.
   _____
   _____

7 I can remember when we *recorded* programmes onto video cassettes.
   _____
   _____

8 What programmes *did you enjoy* as a child?
   _____
   _____

Grammar 4
Past and present tenses

Are these sentences about the past or the present? Tick (✔) your answers.

		Past	Present
1	Sony sold the first Walkman in 1979.		
2	Nowadays, that first Walkman looks really big to us.		
3	But before that, audio cassette players used to be too big to carry around easily.		
4	By the 1990s, portable CD players were also popular.		
5	But of course, you need to use CDs with a portable CD player.		
6	And most people didn't want to carry lots of CDs around with them.		
7	So, on a long journey, you used to listen to the same album over and over.		
8	By the end of the 90s, people were starting to download music from the internet.		
9	Nowadays, many people listen to music on tiny MP3 players.		
10	You just put all your music on your MP3 player.		
11	Many MP3 players store thousands of songs.		

Vocabulary 1
Works of art

Match 1–5 and a–e to make sentences.

1 Van Gogh painted many self-portraits   ____
2 None of the original manuscripts of   ____
3 A huge statue of Christ   ____
4 Leonardo Da Vinci made sketches of   ____
5 There are reproductions of Monet's   ____

a Shakespeare's plays have survived
b painting, *Water Lilies*, on walls around the world
c a flying machine like a helicopter.
d giving us a clear idea of what the artist looked like.
e stands above Rio de Janeiro in Brazil.

Unit 3 Art & Music

Extend your vocabulary 1
discover

Complete the sentences with the words in the box.

| discoveries | discovered | discovers |
| discovery | undiscovered | |

1 Scottish scientist Alexander Fleming _____ penicillin in 1928.
2 The book is about a young boy who _____ a secret door.
3 *New Scientist* magazine publishes news of the latest scientific _____.
4 We're always looking for new _____ musicians.
5 The _____ of water on Mars caused great excitement among scientists.

Vocabulary 2
Furniture and furnishings

Rearrange the letters to make the correct words.

1 h a r i c m a r
_____

2 f a o s
_____

3 p a l m
_____

4 r i r o r m
_____

5 h e f s l
_____

6 r a c i t u n
_____

Extend your vocabulary
Using *just*

Are these sentences correct or incorrect? Circle your answer.

1 The picture looks just right on that wall. *Correct / Incorrect*
2 Don't get just angry, it was a joke. *Correct / Incorrect*
3 Boys, just sit down and be quiet for a moment! *Correct / Incorrect*
4 The film was just like all his others. *Correct / Incorrect*
5 A nice hot drink was what just I needed. *Correct / Incorrect*
6 I just don't like modern art. *Correct / Incorrect*

Vocabulary 3
Music

Complete the sentences with the words in the box.

| group | concert | drummer | guitarist |
| orchestra | singer | musicians | audience |

1 An _____ is a large group of classical _____ who play together.
2 The person who sings in a pop _____ is called a _____.
3 The people who go to a _____ for a performance are called the _____.
4 A person who plays the drums is called a _____ and someone who plays the guitar is a _____.

Vocabulary 4
Audio & video

Complete the texts with the correct words.

When I'm out and about, I usually listen to music on my MP3 (1) *machine / player / play*. You'll often see me walking down the street wearing my (2) *earphones / earpods / soundphones*. If I need to speak to someone, I just (3) *press / make / put* the pause (4) *key / plug / button* so I can hear them.

As a journalist, I still (5) *register / record / wind* most interviews on audio (6) *box / cassette / cast*. Then when I play the interview back later, I can easily (7) *rewind / return / back* the tape if I want to listen again or fast (8) *ahead / eject / forward* through the boring parts.

Unit 3 Art & Music

Vocabulary 5A
Feelings

Write the words in the box under the correct heading below. Do they describe positive or negative feelings?

angry	anxious	bored	calm	cheerful	excited
happy	miserable	relaxed	sad	scared	tense

Positive ☺	Negative ☹

Vocabulary 5B
Feelings

Complete the words in the sentences to describe feelings.

I hate grey, (1) m_____ weather. A bit of sunshine always makes me feel more (2) c_____.

I'm feeling very (3) e_____ about going on holiday next week. I'm a bit (4) a_____ about the journey though because I'm (5) s_____ of flying.

On long journeys, children often get (6) b_____. They behave badly and their parents get (7) a_____ with them.

At the end of a busy day, I often feel (8) t_____. A nice hot bath helps me feel more (9) r_____.

Vocabulary 6
Films

Match the types of film 1–6 to the comments a–f.

1 comedy   a 'I was really scared. I had to cover my eyes a couple of times.'

2 science-fiction   b 'I loved the film. I came out of the cinema still singing the songs!'

3 horror   c 'The film is set in the future, with great special effects.'

4 action   d 'It really made me laugh. The main character was so funny.'

5 musical   e 'It was very tense towards the end. I was on the edge of my seat!'

6 thriller   f 'It was very exciting. Great fight scenes, lots of fast cars.'

Pronunciation 1
Past simple regular verbs

🔊 1.07 Listen and put the past simple forms in the correct column.

asked	decided	hated	listened
looked	needed	opened	started
stopped	walked	wanted	worked

/t/ or /d/	/ɪd/

Pronunciation 2
Used to

🔊 1.08 Listen and underline the stressed words in the sentences.

1 My family used to live in Africa.
2 I used to walk miles to school.
3 We didn't use to have electricity.
4 My mother used to collect water from the river.
5 She used to sing while she worked

Listening
Art curator

🔊 1.09 Listen to someone talking about his job as an art curator. Put these events in the correct order.

____ He spent a year in Italy.
____ He became interested in art.
____ He works as an art curator at a large gallery.
____ He worked as an art researcher.
____ He enjoyed painting pictures when he was young.
____ He studied Art History at university.

Unit 3 Art & Music

Reading
El Sistema

1 Read the article about *El Sistema* and answer the questions.

1 What is *El Sistema*?
_____
_____
_____

2 Where is it?
_____
_____
_____

3 Who is it for?
_____
_____
_____

2 Read the article again and complete these sentences using one word only.

1 *El sistema* was set up in the _____.
2 It helps children from poor areas to escape _____ problems.
3 The children get free _____ instruments and free teaching.
4 Thousands of children in Venezuela play in _____ orchestras.
5 There are now many _____ projects in other countries around the world.

3 Find words in the text with these meanings:

1 teaching (paragraph 1) _____
2 fighting (paragraph 1) _____
3 area (paragraph 2) _____
4 unfair differences (paragraph 2) _____
5 in other places (paragraph 3) _____

4 Without looking at the article, complete the text with the past simple forms of the verbs in the box.

| be | begin | find | see | set | want |
| try | do not | | | | |

Jose Antonio Abreu started *El Sistema* in 1975. He (1) _____ with just eight young musicians, but he soon (2) _____ more young people in Caracas and other cities to join his youth orchestra. He (3) _____ just _____ children from rich families, but he (4) _____ to get kids from some of the poorest districts to get involved in music. Abreu is not only a musician, but also an economist. He (5) _____ up *El Sistema* because he (6) _____ worried about the social inequalities he (7) _____ in his country. He (8) _____ to use music to change lives.

El Sistema: Changing lives through music

A music project in Venezuela changes the lives of thousands of children every year. *El Sistema* offers free musical instruments and tuition to children all over the country at special centres. It offers a chance for poor children to escape from social problems. Around 275,000 children go to these after-school centres, and this keeps many of them away from drugs, alcohol and street violence.

Jose Antonio Abreu started *El Sistema* in 1975. He began with just eight young musicians, but he soon found more young people in Caracas and other cities to join his youth orchestra. He didn't just take children from rich families, but he tried to get kids from some of the poorest districts to get involved in music. Abreu is not only a musician, but also an economist. He set up *El Sistema* because he was worried about the social inequalities he saw in his country. He wanted to use music to change lives.

As well as the after-school centres, *El Sistema* now has 125 youth orchestras, including the Simón Bolívar Youth Orchestra of Venezuela, which plays to audiences around the world. The idea has now been copied to set up similar projects in other South American countries and elsewhere around the world.

Glossary

inequality *(noun)* an unfair situation in which some people have more opportunities, power or money than other people

tuition *(noun)* the work that a teacher does when they teach an individual person or a small group

Art & Music

Writing
Describing a book

1 Reading
How do you decide what books to read? Tick (✔) your answers.

Recommendations from friends. _____

Reviews in newspapers, online, etc. _____

The author's reputation. _____

The design of the book cover. _____

The information on the back of the book. _____

2 The information on the back of a book, sometimes called the *blurb*, tells you something about the book. Read the blurb below and tick (✔) the things it describes.

1 Why the book is popular _____
2 Information about the author _____
3 Where the book is set _____
4 Who the book is about _____
5 What happens in the story _____
6 The ending of the story _____

> ### *Wuthering Heights* by Emily Brontë
> Emily Brontë only wrote one novel and it has become one of the best loved stories in English Literature.
> On the harsh Yorkshire moors, the passionate and violent story of two generations of the Earnshaw and Linton families plays itself out. Orphan Heathcliff falls in love with the wild Cathy and when she will not marry him, terrible things happen to the whole family. But still their love will not die. One of the most famous love stories ever written.

Vocabulary

3 A blurb usually includes plenty of adjectives to make the book sound interesting. Complete the blurb with the adjectives from the box.

clever exciting popular sad successful unhappy

Of Mice and Men by John Steinbeck

The (1) _____ story of George and Lennie, who move from one farm to another, looking for work. George is (2) _____, but Lennie's size and slowness are always getting him into trouble. One day the two men get a job on a farm. Things are going well until they meet the (3) _____ wife of the foreman, Curley. Then Curley's wife tries to become friendly with Lennie …

This (4) _____ story of two outsiders trying to find their place in the world deals with the universal themes of friendship and society. It is one of Steinbeck's most (5) _____ novels and several (6) _____ films have been made of the story.

4 Put the words below into groups with a similar meaning. Check any words you don't know in a dictionary.

| author   book   novel   plot   popular |
story   tale   well-loved   writer

Group 1:
_____
_____

Group 2:
_____
_____

Group 3:
_____
_____

Group 4:
_____
_____

Unit 3 Art & Music

Writing

5 Write a blurb for the back cover of a novel you have read.

Say why the book is interesting and use adjectives to attract readers.

Give a general outline of the story, but remember you don't need a lot of details and don't give away the ending!

Note: The outline of the story is usually written in the present simple.

Useful language

- This is the story of …
- The novel is set in (place) …
- The book tells the story of …
- The main character is …
- a passionate love story
- a gripping thriller
- a murder mystery
- a science-fiction adventure

UNIT 4 Hopes & Fears

Grammar 1A
Future hopes & plans

Are the sentences correct or incorrect? Circle your answer.

1. I hope to get a good job after university.
   Correct / Incorrect
2. I want work for a big international company.
   Correct / Incorrect
3. I'd like doing something in finance.
   Correct / Incorrect
4. My boyfriend and I plan to get married next year.
   Correct / Incorrect
5. We're going to invite all our friends and family.
   Correct / Incorrect
6. I'm looking forward to find a wedding dress.
   Correct / Incorrect
7. I like to have children one day.
   Correct / Incorrect
8. I want to start my career first though.
   Correct / Incorrect

Grammar 1B
Future hopes & plans

Complete these sentences with the correct form of the verbs in brackets.

1. My company _____ (*plan / open*) a new office in Australia soon.
2. I'm _____ (*going to / apply*) for a transfer.
3. I _____ (*hope / get*) a position there for 12 months.
4. I'd _____ (*like / live*) in a different country for a while.
5. I _____ (*want / experience*) a different culture.
6. I'm already _____ (*look forward to / go*) to the beach after work!

Grammar 2
Future plans & intentions

Choose the correct future forms to complete the conversation.

A: (1) *Are you going to / Do you go to* the conference next month?
B: Yes, (2) *I'm doing / I'm going do* a presentation on Tuesday morning.
A: Oh, really? Where (3) *are you staying / you are staying*?
B: I've got a hotel booked near the conference centre.
A: Me too. How (4) *do you getting / are you getting* there?
B: I think (5) *I getting / I'm going to get* the train.
A: (6) *I'm driving / I'm going drive* down on Monday morning. Would you like a lift?
B: Oh, yes please. (7) *Do you going to stay / Are you going to stay* all week
A: No, I've got a meeting on Friday, so (8) *I'm going to come / I'd coming* back on Thursday evening.

Grammar 3
Prediction & ability (*will, be able to*)

Complete the predictions with the future simple form of the verbs in brackets. Use short forms where possible.

'Computer communications (1) _____ (*get*) much faster around the world.'

'Even people in remote areas (2) _____ (*be able to / access*) the internet.'

'All technology (3) _____ (*be*) wireless, so we (4) _____ (*not need*) to plug anything in.

'We (5) _____ (*not use*) keyboards, because users (6) _____ (*be able to / talk*) to their computers.

'Computers (7) _____ (*be able / translate*) from any language to any other instantly.'

'Computer security (8) _____ (*improve*) so that hackers (9) _____ (*not be able to / steal*) your personal information.

Unit 4 Hopes & Fears

Grammar 4
Future time clauses

Complete the sentences with the correct form of the verb.

What will happen in my driving test?

When (1) *you arrive / you'll arrive* at the driving test centre, (2) *you meet / you'll meet* your examiner.

(3) *He goes / He'll go* through some information with you before (4) *you start / you'll start* the test.

When (5) *you get / you'll get* in the car, (6) *he tells / he'll tell* you where to go.

(7) *You are / You'll be* out for about 30 minutes and the examiner (8) *asks / will ask* you to perform some tasks.

If (9) *you make / you'll make* any mistakes, (10) *you lose / you'll lose* marks.

The examiner (11) *tells / will tell* you the final result after (12) *you get / you'll get* back to the test centre.

Grammar 5A
Mixed future forms

Match the underlined verb forms in sentences 1–7 to the tenses and uses a–g.

1 We're having a party next weekend. ____
2 We're going to have a barbecue in the garden. ____
3 We plan to put a big table on the terrace. ____
4 If it rains, we'll have to eat indoors. ____
5 I'm sure it'll be a lovely day. ____
6 And we'll be able to sit out in the garden. ____
7 But I'll check the forecast before we move the table. ____

a present simple after *if*
b future simple for a prediction
c *going to* for an intention
d present simple after *before*
e present verb + infinitive with *to* for a plan
f present continuous for a definite plan
g *will be able to* for a future possibility

Grammar 5B
Mixed future forms

There is one word missing in each sentence. Complete the sentences with the words in the box.

| are | be | to | we'll |

A: Where you going on holiday this year?
B: We plan go to the coast. We'd like stay near the beach. So the boys will able to go surfing.
A: Are you going stay in a hotel?
B: No, probably rent a cottage.

Vocabulary 1A
Adjectives & synonyms

Underline the adjective with a different meaning.

1 good-looking   handsome   beautiful   wonderful
2 intelligent   excellent   clever   smart
3 rich   happy   well-off   wealthy
4 terrible   awful   tense   bad
5 miserable   good   excellent   wonderful

Vocabulary 1B
Adjectives & synonyms

Complete the sentences with the correct adjective.

1 I'm sure you'll have a *wonderful / beautiful* time on holiday.
2 I hope nothing *smart / bad* happens to my family.
3 I'd like to be *well-off / well-up* and live in a *rich / beautiful* house in the countryside.
4 I want to meet a tall, *well-looking / good-looking* man who's *intelligent / handsome* too!
5 She is a very *excellent / clever* student and always gets good marks.

4 Hopes & Fears

Vocabulary 2A
Global issues

Write the phrases in the box under the correct heading below.

| carbon emissions   climate change |
| crime   earthquakes   floods |
| homelessness   pollution   poverty |

Natural disasters	Environmental issues	Social issues

Vocabulary 2B
Global issues

Complete the texts with the words in the box.

| aid   climate   earthquakes   efficient |
| emissions   environmental   natural   war |

We're an international charity and we provide emergency (1) _____ to people around the world. We help people affected by (2) _____ disasters, such as (3) _____. We also help refugees who have left their homes because of (4) _____.

Our organisation provides information about (5) _____ issues such as (6) _____ change. We want to reduce carbon (7) _____ worldwide. We tell people how they can use less electricity and be more energy (8) _____.

Vocabulary 3
Phrasal verbs with *get*

Complete the phrasal verbs with the words in the box.

| around   away   back   together   up |

1 When you sit in traffic on your way home from work, you get _____ feeling tense and tired.
2 In the future, I think more people will get _____ by bike, especially in cities.
3 I like to get _____ on holiday, but I worry about the effect of flying on my carbon footprint.
4 Nowadays, I take time off work and stay at home. I get _____ late and do things locally or I get _____ with my friends and family

Vocabulary 4
Get: meanings and phrases

Tick (✔) the correct meaning of *get* in these sentences.

		become	receive	arrive
1	Scientists say the weather will get warmer in the future.			
2	We'll probably get all our news on our mobile phones.			
3	I'm sure air travel will get quicker.			
4	You'll be able to get from Paris to New York in a couple of hours.			
5	I'm sure cars will get more expensive.			
6	More people will get to work by public transport or on foot.			
7	I think we'll get more energy from wind power.			
8	I hope more people will get proper health care.			

4 Hopes & Fears

Vocabulary 5
Geographical features

Complete the descriptions under these pictures.

1 a l_____   2 a r_____

3 a d_____   4 m_____

5 a f_____   6 the o_____

Extend your vocabulary
-ed / -ing adjectives

Complete the sentences with the correct word.

1 Many people are *worried / worrying* about crime among young people.
2 Teenagers often get into trouble because they're *bored / boring* and have nothing else to do.
3 A *surprised / surprising* number of people are homeless in the city.
4 Politicians are getting more *interested / interesting* in green issues.
5 An earthquake is a *terrified / terrifying* experience.
6 During the war, people were too *frightened / frightening* to leave their homes.
7 The refugees were cold, hungry and *tired / tiring*.
8 There were some *amazed / amazing* pictures of the flood.

Pronunciation 1
Word stress

🔊 **1.10** Listen and put these words in the table according to their stress.

disease	energy	efficient	footprint
recycle	hunger	issue	poverty
pollution			

oO	Oo	Ooo	oOo

Unit 4 Hopes & Fears

Pronunciation 2
Homographs

🔊 **1.11** Some words have the same spelling, but different meanings and pronunciations. These are called *homographs*. Listen and choose the correct pronunciation of the words in bold.

| /red/ | /riːd/ | /tɪə(r)z/ | /teə(r)z/ | /kləʊz/ |
| /kləʊs/ | /lɪvz/ | /laɪvz/ | | |

1 I **read** an interesting story in the newspaper yesterday.
  /red/
  /riːd/
2 I'd like to **read** his latest book.
  /red/
  /riːd/
3 The girl looked so sad, **tears** were running down her face.
  /tɪə(r)z/
  /teə(r)z/
4 The paper is very thin, so it **tears** very easily.
  /tɪə(r)z/
  /teə(r)z/
5 Always **close** your curtains to keep the heat inside.
  /kləʊs/
  /kləʊz/
6 The office is quite **close** to the station.
  /kləʊs/
  /kləʊz/
7 Marisa **lives** in a small village in the mountains.
  /laɪvz/
  /lɪvz/
8 This drug will improve the **lives** of thousands of people.
  /laɪvz/
  /lɪvz/

Listening
Radio interview with an architect

🔊 **1.12** Listen to an architect talking about eco-homes and answer the questions.

1 What is a net-zero carbon home?
  a It doesn't use any energy.
  b It is very energy efficient.
  c It produces as much energy as it uses.
2 How will these houses produce electricity?
  a Using special walls and windows.
  b Using solar panels on the roof.
  c Using an efficient electricity generator.
3 When will people be able to live in these homes?
  a In about one and half years' time.
  b Next month.
  c In eight months' time.
4 What type of homes will the eco-houses be?
  a Large family houses.
  b Small apartments.
  c A mixture of different-sized homes.
5 How much are the homes going to cost?
  a Slightly more than an average home.
  b Much more than a normal home.
  c Less than a traditional home.

Unit 4 Hopes & Fears

Reading
An ageing world population

1 Read the article *An ageing world population* quickly and complete these facts.

1 In 1950, _____ per cent of the world's population was aged over 60.
2 By _____, there will be around 2 billion older people in the world.
3 _____ has the world's youngest population.
4 _____ has the world's oldest population.
5 The ageing population will cause many _____ and _____ changes.

2 Read the article again and answer these questions.

1 What are the causes of this trend?
_____
_____
_____

2 What social and economic changes does the article predict for the future?
_____
_____
_____

3 What other changes do you think there will be?
_____
_____
_____

3 Replace the words and phrases in brackets with words from the article.

Businesses are well aware that the population is (1) (getting older) _____ and they want to take advantage of the 'grey pound' (or dollar or euro). Car makers, for example, are already producing cars which are slightly higher off the ground, so that (2) (elderly) _____ people can get in and out more easily. If this (3) (change) _____ towards an older population continues, other 'grey-friendly' products will surely follow. When today's fifty and sixty-somethings (4) (finish work) _____, they will demand products and technologies to suit their needs and lifestyles.

4 What do you think the 'grey pound' means?
_____
_____
_____

5 Complete the predictions with the verbs in the box. You may use a verb more than once.

| be employ retire use work |

In the future ...

1 many people _____ longer.
2 people _____ at 60 or 65.
3 companies _____ more older workers.
4 old people _____ more active in society.
5 fashion magazines _____ older models.
6 adverts _____ full of young people.

30 Unit 4

Hopes & Fears

An ageing world population

According to the United Nations Population Division, the world population is getting older. In many developed countries, there are already more older people (over 60) than there are children (under 15). They predict that by 2047, the number of older people in the world will be higher than the number of children. In 1950, only 8 per cent of the global population was over 60. By 2007, this figure was 11 per cent and by 2050 it will be 22 per cent. That means that there will be around 2 billion older people in the world. The reasons for this change are simple; people are living longer and families are having fewer children.

There are, of course, big differences between countries. The country with the youngest population is Uganda, with an average age of just 15 years. That is, half the country's population is under 15 and half is over 15. Japan has the oldest population, with an average age of 43 years and about one in five of the population over 60.

Japan is already experiencing very large social and economic changes because of this ageing population. This will cause problems for many societies in the years ahead. With more older people to support, people of working age will have to pay more in taxes to pay for pensions and to care for the elderly. We will need more healthcare workers and fewer teachers. In some countries, people are already planning to retire later. How else will an ageing population change the world we live in? How will it affect our family relationships and the way we think of older people?

Glossary

developed country (*noun*) – a country that has a lot of industries

predict (*verb*) – to say what you think will happen in the future

UNIT 4 Hopes & Fears

Writing
Making arrangements

Reading

1 Read the email below. Do you think that Max and Damien are …

a friends?
b family?
c work colleagues?

> Dear Max,
>
> I'm just writing to check your travel plans for your visit next week.
>
> What time's your flight due to arrive? The airport is just outside the city, so it's probably best to get a taxi to the office. It should cost about €30. Have you got the address?
>
> When you get to the office, I'll introduce you to everyone and go through the schedule for the week. Then I'll take you to your hotel. In the evening, we'll all go out for a meal.
>
> Look forward to seeing you next week.
>
> Best wishes,
>
> Damien

2 Does Damien use any contractions (*I'm*)? Underline them. How would you write these words in full (*I am*)?

Writing skills: formal and informal style

3 Is the language of the email above formal, quite formal or informal? Complete Max's reply with the best phrases using an appropriate style.

(1) *Dear Damien, / Hi!*

(2) *I would like to thank you for your message. / Thanks for your email.*

My flight's due to arrive at 2 o'clock on Monday afternoon. I'll get a taxi from the airport as you suggest. So I hope to be at the office around 3. If my flight's very late, I'll give you a call.

(3) *I'm afraid I don't know the address. / Unfortunately I do not know the address of your office.* Could you email it to me? Thanks!

(4) *See you on Monday / I look forward to meeting you on Monday.*

(5) *Best wishes, / Cheers!*

Max

Writing skills: the time

4 What time is Max's flight due to arrive? What time will he get to the office? There are different ways to write the time. Match the times below.

1 at 2 o'clock on Monday afternoon   a at 16.30
2 around 3   b at 20.00 on Friday
3 at half past four in the afternoon   c about 3pm
4 at quarter to six in the morning   d at 18.04
5 at 8 o'clock on Friday evening   e on Monday at 14.00
6 just after six   f at 5.45am

Language focus: making plans and arrangements

5 Look at the language in the emails for making plans and arrangements.

<u>When you get</u> to the office, <u>I'll introduce</u> you to everyone.
Then <u>I'll take</u> you to your hotel.
In the evening, <u>we'll all go</u> out for a meal.
<u>Look forward to seeing</u> you next week.
My flight <u>is due to arrive</u> at 2 o'clock on Monday afternoon.
<u>I'll get</u> a taxi from the airport.
<u>I hope to be</u> at the office around 3.
<u>If my flight's</u> very late, <u>I'll give</u> you a call.

6 Each sentence below contains one mistake. Find the mistake and correct it.

1 My train is due arrive at 16.30.
2 I'll getting a bus to the city centre.
3 I plan drive to the conference centre.
4 I'll call you when I'll get to the airport.
5 Someone will be meet you at the station.
6 If it will raining, I'll get a taxi.

Writing

5 You are going to a conference in another town for your job. Write an email to a colleague arranging to meet them at the conference. Use the notes below. Then write a suitable reply from your colleague.

- arrive by train, 10am
- taxi to conference centre
- meet Anna at reception desk? 10.30?
- give mobile number – call if late or problems

32   Unit 4

UNIT 5 Work & Leisure

Grammar 1A
have

Underline the main verb in the sentences.

1 My brother has a job with a big multinational company.
2 He has only worked for them for a few months.
3 The company has got offices around the world.
4 He doesn't have his own office yet.
5 He has to work very long hours.
6 He doesn't have much free time anymore.
7 He has a lot of meetings with clients from different countries.
8 He has to speak English a lot for his job.

Grammar 1B
have

Are the sentences correct or incorrect? Circle your answer.

1 Many banks has their main offices in the city centre.
   Correct / Incorrect
2 Most workers have to commute from the suburbs.
   Correct / Incorrect
3 They've to travel for several hours every day.
   Correct / Incorrect
4 On the crowded buses and trains, a lot of people have got to stand.
   Correct / Incorrect
5 Many workers haven't time for a proper lunch break.
   Correct / Incorrect
6 They have to grab a sandwich and eat it at their desk.
   Correct / Incorrect
7 Many offices have their own sandwich shop.
   Correct / Incorrect
8 So staff haven't even to leave the building.
   Correct / Incorrect

Grammar 2A
Modal verbs

Match the modal verbs 1–5 with their meanings a–e.

1 When you join the sports club, you have to fill out a form. ____
2 New members must have an induction before using the gym equipment. ____
3 You can join any of the classes, including yoga, Pilates and aerobics. ____
4 You don't have to wear special clothing, just something comfortable. ____
5 Children under 12 can't use the pool without an adult. ____

a it's possible
b it's necessary
c it isn't necessary
d it's a rule
e it isn't allowed

Grammar 2B
Modal verbs

Complete the sentences with the correct words.

1 Running is great exercise and you *don't have to buy / don't have buy* lots of expensive equipment.
2 You *can running / can run* at any time, you *haven't to sign / don't have to sign* up for a special class.
3 When the weather's bad, you *can always train / can be always training* on a running machine.
4 To run a marathon, you *have to doing / have to do* a lot of training.
5 You *must wear / must to wear* good trainers that fit you properly.
6 You *must not going / mustn't go* out running if you have an injury.

Work & Leisure

Grammar 3A
-ing forms

Use the -ing forms of the verbs in the box to label the activities.

| cook   cycle   jog   ski   snowboard   swim |

1 _____ 2 _____

3 _____ 4 _____

5 _____ 6 _____

Grammar 3B
-ing forms

Complete the job profile with the correct form of the verbs in the box.

| do   enjoy   learn   mind   sit   stand   work   write |

1 You're good at _____ as part of a team.
2 You _____ meeting people.
3 You're tired of _____ behind a desk all day.
4 You dislike _____ the same things every day.
5 You don't _____ travelling for work.
6 You're interested in _____ new skills.
7 You can't _____ missing deadlines.
8 _____ for our new travel website might be for you.

Grammar 4A
Present perfect

Complete the sentences with the past participle form of the verbs in brackets.

Odile has (1) _____ (*be*) a midwife for more than ten years and she's (2) _____ (*deliver*) thousands of babies. Several mothers have (3) _____ (*choose*) to call their baby girls Odile after her.

Chet has (4) _____ (*drive*) his truck all over the US, but he's never (5) _____ (*have*) an accident.

As a journalist, Damien has (6) _____ (*meet*) a lot of famous people, he's (7) _____ (*speak*) to top politicians and he's (8) _____ (*write*) stories about important world events.

Work & Leisure

Grammar 4B
Present perfect, *have been* and *have gone*

Complete the conversations with the correct word.

Paul: Have you ever (1) *been / gone* to the States?
Sue: Yes, I visited New York a couple of years ago.

Jose: Hi. Is Jon there?
Maria: No, I'm sorry, he's just (2) *been / gone* out for a few moments. Can you call back in 10 minutes?

Lars: Sandi's on holiday at the moment. She's (3) *been / gone* to Thailand.
Annika: Oh, lovely. Thailand's a great place for a holiday.
Lars: Have you (4) *been / gone* there?
Annika: Yes, I've (5) *been / gone* a couple of times. I love it.

Yasuko: Is Amelie around?
Luigi: No, she's already (6) *been / gone* home. She left about half an hour ago.

Grammar 5
Present perfect and past simple

Complete the dialogue with the past simple or present perfect form of the verbs in brackets. Use contractions where appropriate.

A: (1) _____ (*you / ever / do*) a job that you really hated?
B: Oh yes, (2) _____ (*I / have*) plenty of terrible jobs! When I was a student, (3) _____ (*I / work*) on a farm one summer.
(4) _____ (*I / pick*) fruit for 6 weeks.
(5) _____ (*it / be*) really hard work and so boring.
A: (6) _____ (*I / never / work*) on a farm, but
(7) _____ (*I / do*) some boring jobs too.
When (8) _____ (*I / leave*) college,
(9) _____ (*I / put*) letters in envelopes for a couple of months to earn some money.

Grammar 6
Mixed verb forms

Put the words in the correct order to make sentences.

1 before / you / skied / ever / Have / ?
_____
_____

2 a few times / only / I've / on lower slopes / tried / .
_____
_____

3 never / been / I've / a ski lift / on / .
_____
_____

4 you / good / is / Cycling / for / .
_____
_____

5 the / riding / countryside / enjoy / in / I / .
_____
_____

6 in the city / I / a helmet / cycle / without / don't / wearing / .
_____
_____

7 surfing / anyone / go / Can / ?
_____
_____

8 quite / have / You / to / fit / be / .
_____
_____

9 good / You / a / be / swimmer / must / .
_____
_____

Unit 5 Work & Leisure

Vocabulary 1
Jobs

Complete this puzzle with job names.

Across
5 She helps people who have legal problems. (6)
6 She makes decisions about the country. (10)
7 He works in a school. (7)

Down
1 She writes stories for newspapers. (10)
2 He brings you food in a restaurant. (6)
3 He makes houses, offices, etc. (7)
4 You go to her when you are sick. (6)

Vocabulary 2
Work

Complete this text with the correct words from the box.

| breaks | employ | hours | security |
| shifts | training | wages | workers |

Some international brand names have been criticised for using badly paid workers in developing countries to produce their goods. (1) _____ in their factories often have to work long (2) _____, including night (3) _____, for low (4) _____. They often work in difficult conditions and they can't even take (5) _____ for food or drinks. They have no job (6) _____ and they sometimes lose their jobs because they are too slow or talk too much. These are usually boring, manual jobs and the workers need little (7) _____. Some factories even (8) _____ children.

Extend your vocabulary
work and job

Complete the sentences with *job*, *jobs* or *work*.

1 There isn't much _____ in the area and the _____ available are mostly low paid.
2 More than 80 people applied for a _____ as a shop assistant in a local supermarket.
3 The women get up at 6 every morning and walk to _____ at the factory.
4 Many of the women have to do two _____ to earn enough money.
5 Some mothers go back to _____ when their children start school; most of them have part-time _____.

Vocabulary 3
Work expressions

Complete the sentences with one preposition in each gap.

1 Try not to make personal calls _____ work time, wait until you go _____ your lunch break.
2 You have to fill in a holiday request form if you want to take time _____.
3 Staff mustn't wear jeans, except on dress _____ days.
4 If you can't come _____ work and you have to call _____ sick, please contact your manager as soon as possible.

36 Unit 5

Unit 5 Work & Leisure

Vocabulary 4
Leisure activities

Match 1–5 with a–e to make sentences.

1 I spend a lot of time chatting   ____
2 If the weather's nice, I often do   ____
3 In the summer, we sometimes go   ____
4 I usually watch   ____
5 The kids spend hours playing   ____
6 On long journeys, I usually read   ____
7 When I get home from work, I cook   ____
8 My son's very fit. He does   ____

a for a walk in the countryside.
b dinner for the family.
c to friends on my mobile.
d computer games.
e a book to pass the time.
f a lot of sport.
g the gardening at the weekend.
h the news on TV in the evening.

Pronunciation 1
can / can't, must / mustn't

🔊 **1.13** Listen and choose the modal verb form you hear.

1 Employees *can / can't* park in front of the office.
2 You *can / can't* make personal calls from your desk.
3 You *can / can't* work flexible hours.
4 You *must / mustn't* eat breakfast on the morning of the race.
5 You *can / can't* hire surfing equipment at the beach.
6 You *must / mustn't* bring a bag with you.

Pronunciation 2
/ŋ/

🔊 **1.14** Listen and underline the words in these sentences which contain a /ŋ/ sound.

1 Many young people spend their evenings on social networking websites.
2 Fishing is the most popular hobby in England.
3 On holiday, a lot of people like sitting on the beach, reading a book or just doing nothing.
4 Some people enjoy collecting things, such as stamps or coins.
5 Surfing and skiing are popular sports with young people.

Pronunciation 3
Past participles

🔊 **1.15** Listen and underline the past participle with a different vowel sound.

1	bought	taught	got	thought
2	won	gone	done	begun
3	learnt	meant	sent	spent
4	written	driven	eaten	given
5	read	said	paid	sent

Listening
Leisure and lifestyle

🔊 **1.16** Listen to people talking about leisure activities in different countries and choose the correct country for each statement. Tick (✔) your answers.

		USA	Australia	Canada
1	People spend a lot of their free time at home.			
2	People spend a lot of their free time outdoors.			
3	Winter sports are very popular.			
4	A lot of people enjoy watersports.			
5	Gardening is a popular hobby.			
6	Golf is the most popular sport.			
7	Many parts of the country are very cold.			
8	Most people in the country live near the sea.			

Unit 5 Work & Leisure

Reading
The changing workplace

1 Read the article *Flexible working* quickly. What are *teleworking* and *hot desking*?

2 Read the article again. Tick (✔) the statements that are true.

1 Because of new technology, workers can …
   a more easily work from home.
   b work more hours.
   c stay in contact with work when they are not in the office.
2 Hot desking means that staff don't have to …
   a always work at the same desk.
   b stay in the office all day.
   c work as part of a team.

3 Complete the sentences with phrases from the text.

1 I'm sorry, I'm _____ _____ _____ _____ at the moment. Please leave a message.
2 Many people no longer work _____ _____ _____. Flexible working hours are much more common.
3 I always carry my mobile phone so that I can _____ _____ _____ when I'm out visiting clients.

4 Look at these sentences from the text. Add *have* or *has* to each sentence.

1 The modern office _____ changed rapidly in recent years.
2 Office workers no longer _____ to sit at the same desk from nine to five.
3 One innovation _____ been 'hot desking'.
4 Employees don't _____ their own desk in the office.
5 Companies don't _____ to pay for so much office space.
6 They _____ more freedom to work how and where they want.

5 Mark each sentence in exercise 4 MV (*have* as the main verb), MOD (*have to* as a modal) or AUX (*have* as an auxiliary verb).

Flexible working

The modern office has changed a lot in recent years. New technology now allows people to work in different ways and to be more flexible. Fast internet connections mean that people can work from home. This is sometimes known as *teleworking*. And mobile technology allows everyone to keep in touch while they're out of the office. People can contact you on your mobile or you can check your email on your laptop in a wi-fi hotspot.

Even when they're in the office, workers no longer have to sit at the same desk from nine to five every day. Businesses are rethinking the traditional office and one new idea has been *hot desking*. This is a way of working in which employees don't have their own desk in the office, but use any desk that's available when they come in.

But what are the advantages and disadvantages of flexible working?

On the plus side:
Workers have more freedom to work how and where they like. They can fit their work around their lifestyle. Mothers, for example, can work from home and still be around when the kids get home from school.
Companies don't have to pay for so much office space. Teleworkers don't need desk space and hot desking can cut space by up to 30%, reducing costs.

On the down side:
Spending less time in the office can leave staff feeling that they don't belong. Team spirit can suffer because people don't build relationships with their colleagues.
There are possible health problems too. People who work for a long time at a computer need a comfortable computer set-up. If workers are at home or moving from desk to desk, employers can't check that they're working safely.

Hot desking
Where does the word come from?
The term may be copied from 'hot bunking', a practice in the navy where sailors on different shifts use the same bed (or bunk). When one sailor gets up, another takes his place in the bunk - which is still warm.

Glossary
wi-fi hotspot (*noun*) – a place where you can connect to the internet without wires

Work & Leisure

Writing
A letter of application

Reading

1 Many people work as volunteers *(they work for no payment)*. Where might you find volunteers doing these activities?

1 clearing footpaths

2 visiting elderly people

3 answering visitors' questions

4 helping disabled children

5 showing people to their seats

6 giving out hot drinks

7 planting trees

8 collecting litter

2 Read the advertisement below for volunteers at a zoo and complete these sentences.

1 Volunteers _____ special qualifications.
2 Volunteers _____ interested in animals.
3 Volunteers _____ over 18.
4 Volunteers _____ available at least one day a week.

> The zoo needs volunteers to help out and answer visitors' questions during the busy summer period.
>
> You don't have to have special qualifications as full training will be given, but you must be interested in animals.
>
> Volunteers must be available for at least one day a week and must be over 18.
>
> If you are interested in becoming a volunteer, contact our volunteer manager
>
> Paul Ashton.

Language focus: past simple and present perfect

3 Now read the email in reply to the advertisement. Which tenses does Lisa use in these sentences to talk about her experience? Why?

1 *I've worked* as a volunteer on a number of conservation projects.

2 In 2004, *I spent* 4 weeks helping out at a turtle conservation project in Greece.

3 Last year, *I took part in* a project to protect birds in my local area.

> Dear Mr Ashton,
> I'm getting in touch about your advertisement for volunteers at the zoo.
> I'm very interested in animals and conservation. I've worked as a volunteer on a number of conservation projects. In 2004, I spent 4 weeks helping out at a turtle conservation project in Greece and last year, I took part in a project to protect birds in my local area.
> I would be grateful if you could send me more information about your volunteer programme.
> Yours,
> Lisa Weston.

4 Complete the sentences about work experience using the past simple or present perfect form of the verb in brackets.

1 I _____ (*study*) Biology at university.
2 When I was at university, I _____ (*write*) for the student newspaper.
3 I _____ (*work*) with children for many years.
4 From 2005 to 2007, I _____ (*teach*) English in Japan.
5 I _____ (*take*) a number of computer skills courses.
6 I _____ (*never work*) abroad before.

Unit 5 Work & Leisure

Writing

5 Read the advertisement for volunteers to help at an international sporting event. Use the notes to write an email in reply to the advertisement.

> ## Do you love sport?
> Volunteers are needed for a major international sporting event in July.
>
> Volunteers will collect tickets, show people to their seats and provide information.
>
> You must be good at communicating with people. Foreign language skills are an advantage.
>
> You must be available from 5-9 July.
>
> Volunteers must be over 18.
>
> If you can help, please contact the events manager, George Ellis, for more information.

> *Interests: all sports, especially athletics*
>
> *Language skills: excellent English, good Spanish, some French*
>
> *Experience: work at other international events, ticket sales at Expo07, tour guide at local museum last summer*
>
> *Enjoy meeting people*
>
> *Available in July*

UNIT 6 Science & Technology

Grammar 1A
Comparatives

Complete the facts with the correct words.

Did you know?

Carbon dioxide is (1) *heavyer / heavier* than air.

Light travels (2) *slower / more slowly* through water than through air, but sound travels (3) *more fastly / faster*.

The air at the top of Mount Everest is three times (4) *thiner / thinner* than at sea level.

The wingspan of a Boeing 747 is (5) *longer / more long* than the Wright brothers' first aeroplane.

People are slightly (6) *more tall / taller* in space because there's no gravity pulling them down.

A dog's sense of smell is 1,000 times (7) *more sensitive / sensitiver* than a person's.

Kiwi fruit are (8) *healther / healthier* than oranges, because they contain twice as much vitamin C.

Grammar 1B
Comparative adjectives

Complete the sentences with the comparative form of the underlined adjective.

1. French TGV trains are <u>fast</u>, but the Japanese bullet train is _____.
2. The Empire State building is very <u>tall</u>, but Taipei 101 is _____.
3. The traffic in Los Angeles is <u>bad</u>, but it's even _____ in São Paolo.
4. Tokyo is an <u>expensive</u> city to live in, but London is even _____.
5. England is a pretty <u>wet</u> country, but apparently, Hawaii is _____.
6. Australia is a <u>dry</u> country, but Egypt is _____.
7. The Atlantic ocean is very <u>large</u>, but the Pacific is _____.
8. India has a very <u>big</u> population, but the population of China is even _____.
9. Spain is <u>popular</u> with international tourists, but France is _____.

Grammar 1C
Comparative adverbs

Complete the sentences with the comparative form of the adverb in brackets.

1. Computers can do many jobs _____ (*quickly*) and _____ (*efficiently*) than people.
2. Using the internet, people can find information _____ (*easily*) than in the past.
3. People with IT skills are often paid _____ (*well*) than those without.
4. A computer can do calculations much _____ (*fast*) than a human being.
5. Children who grow up using computers do _____ (*badly*) in maths tests than people from older generations.

Grammar 2
Comparatives *(a bit, much, (not) as ... as)*

Put the words in order to make sentences.

1. lifestyle / simpler / ours / My grandparents' / much / was / than / .
   _____
   _____
2. worked / do / as hard / just / we / as / They / .
   _____
   _____
3. slowly / happened / in those days / more / Things / much / .
   _____
   _____
4. lifestyles / stressful as / So people's / weren't / as / ours / .
   _____
   _____

Unit 6 41

6 Science & Technology

5 than / were / probably / They / people nowadays / fitter / a bit / .
_____
_____
_____

6 further / we / They / walk / do / had to / than / much / .
_____
_____
_____

7 weren't / are / as healthy / as / we / But they / .
_____
_____
_____

8 People / to die of / much / were / likely / more / common diseases / .
_____
_____
_____

Grammar 3
Superlatives

Complete the sentences with the superlative form of the adjectives in the box.

| cold | dangerous | deep | dry |
| heavy | large | loud | popular |

1 The call of the humpback whale is _____ sound made by any living creature.
2 Statistically, the mosquito is _____ animal in the world, killing 2–3 million people a year.
3 Across the world, dogs are _____ animals to keep as pets.
4 Male African elephants are _____ land animals on Earth.
5 Antarctica is _____ of the world's continents.
6 The Sahara stretches across more than ten countries and is _____ desert in the world.
7 _____ place in the world's oceans is the Mariana trench in the Pacific.
8 Aswan, in Egypt is _____ inhabited place in the world.

Grammar 4
Phrasal verbs and objects

Underline the phrases which are incorrect.

First, (1) *switch on your camera* and (2) *plug it into your computer* using the special lead.

When your photos are downloaded, you can unplug the camera and (3) *switch off it*.

Now you can send your photos to your friends or (4) *print out them*.

To label your photos, just (5) *click on the file name* and (6) *type a new name in*.

If your camera battery is low, (7) *take out it* and (8) *charge up it* using the charger provided.

Vocabulary 1A
Adjectives

Match these adjectives with their opposite meanings.

1 safe   a relaxing
2 rich   b expensive
3 interesting   c dangerous
4 weak   d relaxed
5 easy   e boring
6 cheap   f difficult
7 stressful   g strong
8 nervous   h poor

Science & Technology

Vocabulary 1B
Adjectives

Complete the text with the adjectives in the box.

| cheaper | easier | nervous | popular |
| safer | satisfied | stressful | wider |

Online shopping has become more and more
(1) _____ in recent years. Some people shop
online because things are often (2) _____ than
in the shops and you have a (3) _____ choice
of goods. Others just find it less (4) _____ than
pushing through the crowds in the shops. Some people are
(5) _____ about using their credit cards online,
but experts say it's (6) _____ than handing your
card to a stranger in a shop. And if you're not
(7) _____ with the goods when they arrive, you
can just send them back. It couldn't be (8) _____.

Extend your vocabulary 1
Metaphors for happiness

Complete the expressions with words from the box.

| air | down | heart | spirits | top |

1 The bright sunny weather lifted her _____.
2 Are you alright? You look a little _____.
3 Her _____ sank as she read the letter.
4 She was on _____ of the world after getting a place at university.
5 He was still walking on _____ from his meeting with Anna.

Vocabulary 2
Noun formation

Complete these sentences with the correct noun form of the word in brackets.

1 Suzy received a _____ (*scholar*) to pay for her university studies.
2 She studied Chemistry then got a job as a research _____ (*science*).
3 Luke started his career as a science _____ (*teach*) in a school.
4 He changed jobs and became a _____ (*research*) for an aerospace company.
5 He tests the metal used in planes to check for any _____ (*weak*).
6 Magda is an _____ (*economy*) for an international bank.
7 She's interested in the _____ (*relation*) between aid and economic development.

Extend your vocabulary 2
Other ways of saying *yes*

🔊 1.17 Listen and complete this conversation with the replies in the box.

| Definitely | I'm afraid so | OK |
| That's right | Yep | |

Computer user: My computer's stopped working. When I click on the screen, nothing happens.
Engineer: Nothing happens at all?
Computer user: (1) _____.
Engineer: Have you tried using the keyboard instead?
Computer user: (2) _____. Still nothing.
Engineer: I think we'll have to shut down and start again.
Computer user: (3) _____. But won't I lose what I was working on?
Engineer: (4) _____. When did you last save your work?
Computer user: Oh, a few minutes ago.
Engineer: Are you sure?
Computer user: (5) _____.
Engineer: Then you won't lose too much.

6 Science & Technology

Vocabulary 3
Compound nouns

Complete the names of the items in the pictures.

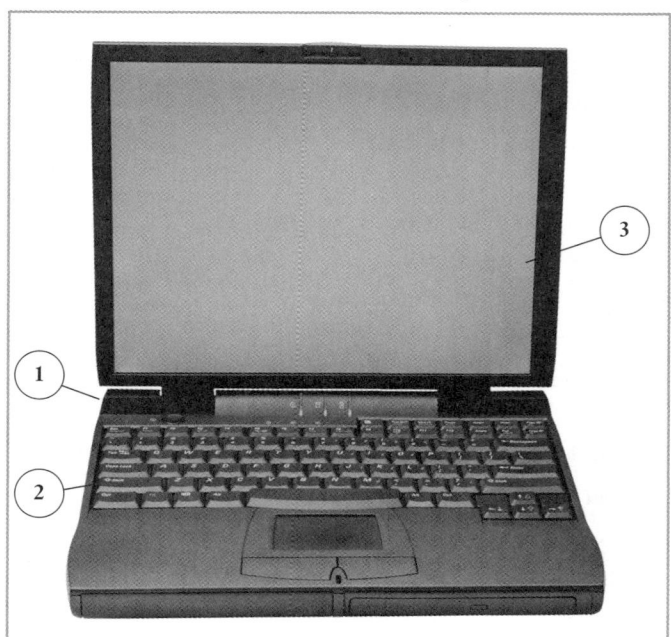

1 l_____
2 k_____
3 c_____ s_____

4 h_____

5 m_____ p_____
6 t_____ m_____

Vocabulary 4A
Phrasal verbs

Match 1–8 and a–h to make questions.

1   Why don't you just pick   _____
2   Have you plugged   _____
3   Why don't you print   _____
4   Could you turn   _____
5   Can you shut   _____
6   Did you type   _____
7   Why don't you log   _____
8   Has the whole system gone   _____

a   the power cable in?
b   on and check your email now?
c   up the phone and call them?
d   down the computer when you've finished?
e   out the map to take with you?
f   down?
g   the sound down a bit?
h   your password in correctly?

Science & Technology

Vocabulary 4B
Phrasal verbs

Complete these sentences with the correct preposition (*up*, *in*, *on*, etc).

1 She picked _____ the phone and dialled his number.
2 Yes, I definitely plugged the power cable _____.
3 He printed _____ the map from the website.
4 It was a bit too loud, so I turned the sound _____.
5 He shut the computer _____ and switched _____ the lights before he left.
6 I'm sure I typed _____ my password correctly.
7 Do I need a password to log _____?
8 Yes, the whole computer system has gone _____. Nothing's working.

Vocabulary 5
Finding things in common

Complete the facts with the correct phrases.

1 Scientist, Charles Darwin was born on 12th of February 1809. *So was / Neither was* American president, Abraham Lincoln.
2 The Scottish biologist, Alexander Fleming won a Nobel Prize for his work. *So did / So is* the Polish chemist, Marie Curie
3 Switzerland has no sea coast. *So has / Neither has* Austria.
4 China has a population of more than 1 billion people. *Does so / So does* India.
5 'I really like dogs.'
  'Me *too / neither*.'
6 Snakes don't have ears. *Neither do / So don't* spiders.

Pronunciation 1
schwa /ə/

🔊 **1.18** Listen and circle the word with the underlined sound that is not schwa /ə/.

1 teach<u>e</u>r   doct<u>o</u>r   manag<u>e</u>r   engin<u>ee</u>r
2 fitt<u>e</u>r   f<u>a</u>r   bett<u>e</u>r   popul<u>a</u>r
3 p<u>o</u>rtable   pr<u>o</u>ductive   s<u>u</u>rprising   pati<u>e</u>nt
4 <u>e</u>xercise   pov<u>e</u>rty   int<u>e</u>rview   res<u>ea</u>rch
5 <u>u</u>mbrella   are<u>a</u>   sp<u>a</u>   sof<u>a</u>

Pronunciation 2
Email and website addresses

🔊 **1.19** Listen and complete these website and email addresses.

1 _____.com
2 news._____
3 _____.wikipedia_____
4 _____hotmail.com
5 _____stein_____

Listening
Maths teaching

🔊 **1.20** Listen to a university maths professor talking about maths teaching. Complete the sentences with the correct words.

1 Students are *more interested / less interested* in maths than they used to be.
2 *More / Fewer* students are studying maths at university.
3 It's easier to use a mobile phone than to do a *calculation / calculator* in your head.
4 Some *complex / common* fractions, like ½ and ¼, are still used in everyday life.
5 Fractions were *useful / useless* in the past before we had calculators and computers.
6 Fractions aren't *directly / relevant* to most people in the modern world.
7 He says that teachers should spend *more / less* time teaching fractions at school.

Unit 6 Science & Technology

Reading
The history of computers

1 Look at these dictionary definitions.

> **mini-** *(prefix)* – smaller or shorter than other things of the same kind

> **micro-** *(prefix)* – extremely small: used with some nouns and adjectives

Complete these sentences with *mini* or *micro* and the word in brackets.

1 There was a _____ on TV last week about the invention of the World Wide Web. (*series*)
2 Today, _____ are in all PCs. They were invented in the late 1950s. (*chips*)
3 They've got five children, so they're thinking of buying a _____ (*van*).
4 Some people cook all their food in a _____ oven. (*wave*)

Can you think of any other words which start with *mini-* or *micro-*?

2 Answer the question below. Then read the article *The Dawn of the Digital Age* and check your answer.

Which of these computers is the largest and the smallest?

- a minicomputer
- a microcomputer
- a personal computer (PC)

3 Read the article again and answer the questions.

1 'Baby' was …
  a a very large computer.
  b an extremely small computer.
  c a portable computer.
2 Moore's Law describes how quickly computers become …
  a smaller.
  b more powerful.
  c cheaper.
3 Early PCs stored information on …
  a CDs.
  b memory sticks.
  c cassette tapes.
4 'Windows' made computers …
  a more affordable.
  b easier to use.
  c smaller.
5 The World Wide Web was invented …
  a in the late eighties.
  b in the early eighties.
  c in 1985.

4 The suffix *-able* (or *-ible*) is used to form many adjectives.

> **-able** *(suffix)* – used with many verbs to make adjectives describing something that can be done: *enjoyable* (=that people can enjoy), *breakable* (=that is easy to break)

Find three adjectives in the article that end with *-able*. Match them to these definitions.

1 Easy to carry or move   _____
2 Cheap enough for ordinary people to buy _____
3 That you can find, buy or use   _____

5 Complete the phrases with the correct adjectives from the text.

1 _____ behaviour   behaviour that people can accept
2 an _____ accident an accident that can be avoided
3 a _____ change   a change that people can notice
4 _____ packaging   packaging that can be recycled

6 Complete the sentences with the correct form of the words in brackets. Use extra words if necessary.

1 A PC has become a common piece of equipment in many homes, and _____ (*so*) a wireless modem.
2 With a wireless internet connection you don't need to _____ (*plug into / your computer*) a modem.
3 Although a relatively recent invention, the internet has become one of our _____ (*popular*) pastimes.
4 However, PCs are not selling _____ (*well*) they sold 10 years ago because many people are happy with the one they have.
5 I don't need all the power my PC has, and _____ (*do*) many other people.
6 Laptop computers are _____ (*much / cheap*) now than they were 10 years ago and many people prefer them to desktop PCs.

Science & Technology

The Dawn of the Digital Age

These days computers are everywhere, and we don't really think about them. But they're actually a very recent invention and they have developed very quickly.

1940s

The first real electronic computers were developed in the 1940s. They were huge machines which filled whole rooms at universities and other research facilities. The world's first digital computer that could store programs was called *Baby* and was built at Manchester University in England in 1948.

"Computers in the future may weigh no more than 1.5 tons"
Popular Mechanics magazine, 1949

1950s

During the 1950s, computers first became available to a few large businesses. They were still huge machines, though, and very expensive. They used magnetic tape to input and store data.

1960s

New technology made computers much smaller and much cheaper. The minicomputer became available to even small businesses.

Moore's Law

In 1965, computer scientist Gordon Moore predicted that computers would double in power every two years. Until now, his law has proved to be correct.

1970s

The first microprocessor was launched in 1971 and by the mid-seventies, the first personal computers appeared. These early PCs were still quite large and expensive and used cassette tapes to store data.

1980s

Personal computers became affordable and more widely available. At first, when you switched on your new PC, you got a blank screen with a cursor flashing in the top corner. Then, in 1985, Microsoft launched the Windows operating system, making computing easier for everyone.

By the late eighties, PCs were becoming smaller and more portable and laptops were now available. In 1989, Tim Berners-Lee invented the World Wide Web and the modern digital age really began.

Unit 6 Science & Technology

Writing
Mobile phones

Reading

1 Read the short articles below about mobile phones. Do they talk about advantages or disadvantages?

> Recent research into the use of mobile phones by young people in Bangalore, India, found that mobiles have become essential for personal relationships. Many young people work night shifts in call centres so they use their mobiles to keep in touch with friends, who often work different hours. Many young people leave their home towns and villages to work in Bangalore and they keep in touch with family and even partners by mobile phone.

> University graduates are using text message abbreviations in job applications. Many employers are complaining about the bad spelling and poor grammar of younger employees. They also say that people are used to the friendly style of text messages and they don't know how to use correct, formal English for business communication.

> Two hikers were saved by their mobile phones. They got lost while they were hiking in Alaska. Then one of the women managed to get a signal on her mobile phone and called her mother. Rescue teams spoke to her and she described the landscape around her. The mobile phone company helped too by finding the exact position of her phone. Helicopters searched the area and finally found the two women and took them to safety.

> Train passengers have become so tired of listening to other people talking loudly on their mobile phones, many train companies have introduced *quiet* carriages. On most UK trains, for example, there is a quiet carriage in which passengers are asked to switch off mobile phones and mp3 players. Some train companies are even thinking about having special carriages which stop mobile phone signals.

Glossary
abbreviation (*noun*) – a short form of a word or phrase

Language focus: comparatives and superlatives

2 Complete the comments about mobile phones using the comparative or superlative form of the adjectives in brackets.

The (1) _____ (*annoying*) thing about mobile phones is when people talk really loudly into them on the train.

If you're in a quiet place, like a library or a theatre, it's (2) _____ (*good*) to send a text message than to call someone.

Sometimes it's (3) _____ (*convenient*) to send somebody a text message so that you don't disturb them with a call.

It's (4) _____ (*easy*) to give someone bad news via text message than face to face, but it's also not polite or kind.

One of (5) _____ (*bad*) things about mobile phones is when people keep checking their phone while you're talking to them.

If you're late for a meeting, it's much (6) _____ (*polite*) to send someone a text message to let them know, rather than just leave them waiting.

I feel much (7) _____ (*safe*) driving on my own, because if there's an emergency, I can call someone from the car. I don't have to walk along the road on my own to find a phone box.

Modern mobile phones have so many different features. For me, (8) _____ (*useful*) thing is having a camera in my phone.

Science & Technology

Writing skills: introductions

3 When you write an essay, you need to make your topic clear in your introduction. Which of these things would be suitable for an introduction?

- background to the topic: *mobile phones have become more common across the world*
- general questions: *Are mobile phones bad for society?*
- the situation in your country: *in my country, almost all young people carry a mobile phone*
- detailed examples: *if you are going to be late for a meeting, it's better to ….*
- the topic of the essay: *mobile phones have both advantages and disadvantages*
- your opinion: *I think that mobile phones are essential in the modern world*
- main points: *one of the main advantages of mobile phones is …*

Preparing to write

4 Use the ideas in exercise 3 and your own ideas to make notes about the advantages and disadvantages of mobile phones.

Advantages	Disadvantages
Convenient: *easy to keep in touch*	Annoying:
Safety:	Communication skills: *poor spelling*
Extra features:	

Writing

5 Write an essay about the advantages and disadvantages of mobile phones. Write four paragraphs; introduction, advantages, disadvantages, and conclusion.

Unit 7 Time & Money

Grammar 1A
Present perfect with *for* & *since*

Are these time expressions used with *for* or *since*? Write the phrases in the box under the correct heading below.

4 o'clock	5th June	20 years	1956
a few minutes	a long time	last Friday
several hours	two weeks	the 10th century

for	since

Grammar 1B
Present perfect with *for* & *since*

Complete the sentences with the correct word.

People have used calendars (1) *in / for / since* ancient times to divide the year into days and months. The western calendar, based on the solar cycle, has existed (2) *in / for / since* Roman times. Many European countries have used the modern Gregorian calendar (3) *in / for / since* more than 400 years. Britain adopted it as the official calendar (4) *in / for / since* 1752.

The Islamic calendar has been used by Muslims (5) *in / for / since* the seventh century and has a year that is 11 days shorter than the Gregorian calendar.

The traditional Chinese calendar is based on the cycles of both the sun and the moon and has existed in some form (6) *in / for / since* more than three thousand years. The Gregorian calendar has been the official calendar in China (7) *in / for / since* 1929, but the Chinese calendar is still used for traditional festivals such as the Chinese New Year. For example, (8) *in / for / since* 2010 the Chinese New Year started on February 14.

Grammar 2
Present perfect with *yet* & *already*

Rewrite the sentences with the adverb in brackets.

1 People have travelled into space. (*already*)
___
___

2 Men haven't been to other planets. (*yet*)
___
___

3 Have spacecraft landed on Mars? (*yet*)
___
___

4 Many European countries have adopted the Euro. (*already*)
___
___

5 Has Britain started using the Euro? (*yet*)
___
___

6 Scientists have discovered cures for many diseases. (*already*)
___
___

7 Doctors have managed to transplant all kinds of organs. (*already*)
___
___

8 We haven't found a cure for the common cold. (*yet*)
___
___

Time & Money

Grammar 3
Present perfect and past simple

Choose the sentence that best follows the first one.

1 My family have lived in Britain since the 1950s.
   a   We all live in or around London.
   b   We now live in Canada.
2 My grandmother didn't speak any English when she first arrived.
   a   She doesn't speak English now.
   b   Her English is very good now.
3 She worked in a shop for 20 years.
   a   Now she's retired.
   b   She works there five days a week.
4 She's continued many of the traditions from her home country.
   a   She still follows those traditions.
   b   She doesn't continue those traditions now.
5 She's kept in touch with family in her home country.
   a   She's still in touch with family from home.
   b   She doesn't contact family from home now.
6 For many years, she sent a letter to her sister every week.
   a   She always writes it on a Sunday evening and posts it on a Monday morning.
   b   Now she keeps in touch with her by email.

Vocabulary 1
Prepositions of time *in, on, at*

Complete the text with the correct prepositions.

For the Chinese, the number 8 is a lucky number.
(1) *In / At / On* 2008 the opening ceremony of the Olympic Games in Beijing began (2) *in / at / on* 8.08pm (3) *in / at / on* 8 August (the 8th day of the 8th month). The number 8 was certainly lucky for American swimmer, Michael Phelps. (4) *In / At / On* 17 August he won the last of his 8 gold medals, a new record.

The games took place (5) *in / at / on* summer, but the weather was changeable. There was heavy rain (6) *in / at / on* night for some of the track and field events, and some races, such as the marathon, were held (7) *in / at / on* the early morning because of the heat.

Vocabulary 2
Time crossword

Complete this time puzzle.

Across

3   the shortest month of the year (8)
4   there are four in a year (7)
7   the seventh month of the year (4)
8   the time for new plants and flowers (6)
9   the start of the day (7)

Down

1   the middle of the week (9)
2   the first month of the year (7)
5   the time of day to relax (7)
6   less than a minute (6)
8   the warmest part of the year (6)

Unit 7

Unit 7 Time & Money

Vocabulary 3
Time expressions

Complete the sentences with the correct word.

1 I'll be home late tonight because I've got to work *overtime / extratime*.
2 You usually get jet lag when you travel across several time *areas / zones*.
3 Nowadays, children don't *pass / spend* enough time playing outdoors.
4 To *make / save* time, I heat the milk in the microwave.
5 Diets are a *loss / waste* of time, you always put the weight back on.
6 I don't get much *free / empty* time nowadays. I'm either at work or looking after the family.

Vocabulary 4
Money

Match 1–6 and a–f to make sentences.

1 The hotel didn't take credit cards, ___
2 I haven't got much money with me ___
3 I'm sorry I don't have any change, ___
4 House prices are so high around here ___
5 We both retired a couple of years ago, ___
6 I didn't want to send cash through the post, ___

a just a fifty dollar note.
b so I put a cheque in an envelope.
c so we had to pay in cash.
d so now we live off our pensions.
e just a few coins in my pocket.
f we had to get a huge mortgage.

Vocabulary 5
Money verb phrases

Complete the sentences with the words in the box, you can use the words more than once.

| earn | owe | pay | spend | take |

1 To buy a new car, many people have to _____ out a loan from the bank.
2 Customers have to _____ their bills within 30 days.
3 In most countries, women still don't _____ as much money as men.
4 When many students leave university, they _____ a lot of money to the bank.
5 A lot of families _____ most of their money on food and bills.
6 Most shop workers only _____ the minimum wage.
7 Most people have to _____ out a big mortgage for their first home.
8 How much would you _____ for a pair of sunglasses?

Extend your vocabulary
borrow & lend

Complete the texts with the correct form of *borrow* or *lend*.

Credit unions are organisations that (1) _____ fairly small amounts of money to people in the local community. If people want to (2) _____ money from a credit union, they have to become a member. Unlike a bank, a credit union is owned by its members.

Libraries (3) _____ millions of books to people every year. Usually people can (4) _____ a fixed number of books at a time and they have to return them within a certain period. One sign of a writer's popularity is how many people (5) _____ their books each year. In 2008, the most popular writer in the UK was James Patterson. UK libraries (6) _____ his books more than 1.5 million times. In the US in the same year, people (7) _____ a novel called *The Memory Keeper's Daughter* by Kim Edwards more often than any other book.

Unit 7 Time & Money

Pronunciation 1
/aɪ/ and /eɪ/

1.21 Listen and tick (✔) the vowel sounds in the underlined words.

	/aɪ/	/eɪ/	a different sound
1 <u>nine</u> o'clock at <u>night</u>			
2 hooray, it's <u>pay</u> <u>day</u>			
3 the <u>eighth</u> of <u>May</u>			
4 <u>half</u> <u>past</u> seven			
5 <u>five</u> <u>times</u> a week			
6 <u>six</u> <u>minutes</u> later			

Pronunciation 2
/ʌ/

1.22 Listen and underline the word in each group which does not contain the /ʌ/ sound.

1	money	Monday	mortgage	month
2	bus	buy	but	button
3	some	sun	one	home
4	house	young	couple	country
5	brother	another	both	mother
6	done	fun	won	alone

Listening
The history of money

1 **1.23** Listen to *The history of money* and match the types of money 1–7 to the time periods a–g.

1. early humans
2. 3,000 years ago
3. 500 BC
4. 2,000 years ago
5. 9th century
6. 1816
7. today

a. first metal currency
b. first banknotes
c. electronic money
d. barter system
e. gold standard
f. first gold and silver coins
g. first paper currency

2 **1.23** Listen again and choose the correct words to complete these sentences.

1. The first coins had a *hole / chain / vegetable* in the middle.
2. The first banknotes were made of *paper / leather / silver*.
3. The Chinese first used paper currency *after / before / the same time as* the Europeans did.
4. There were economic problems in *500 BC / 1816 / the 1930s*.
5. The gold standard was introduced to try to control *inflation / the Chinese / the price of gold*.

Unit 7 Time & Money

Reading
A cashless society

1 Read the article *Is cash going out of fashion?* What is a 'cashless society'?

_____
_____
_____

2 Read the article again and answer the questions.

1 What is the most popular way to pay for small things that we buy?

_____
_____
_____

2 What percentage of transactions are in cash in countries like the UK?

_____
_____
_____

3 How does contactless technology use mobile phones?

_____
_____
_____

4 Which country has already started to use the new technology?

_____
_____
_____

5 Why will this technology take time to spread to other countries?

_____
_____
_____

Vocabulary

3 Find words in the text to match these definitions.

1 _____ money in the form of notes and coins
2 _____ a small plastic card that you use to buy things now and pay for them later
3 _____ a plastic card that you use to pay for things directly from your bank account
4 _____ flat round pieces of metal used as money
5 _____ personal identification number
6 _____ something that you buy
7 _____ the process of buying or selling something

4 Complete the expressions from the text with one preposition or particle in each space.

1 I don't think cash will go _____ of fashion for a long time.
2 I think we'll always use cash to pay _____ things at market stalls and places like that.
3 For little things, it's just much easier to pay _____ cash.
4 It's easier to hand _____ your credit card than to carry _____ lots of cash.
5 At the moment, you put your card in a reader, then you type _____ your PIN.

Time & Money

Is cash going out of fashion?

New technology may mean that we are getting closer to a cashless society. We are now used to paying for many things with cards instead of cash. It's now common around the world to hand over your debit or credit card in shops, hotels and restaurants. You put your card in a reader, type in your PIN and that's it. It's simpler and safer than carrying around large amounts of cash. Cash is still more popular for small purchases though. If you're buying a newspaper or a cup of coffee, you'll probably pay by cash. Even in developed countries such as the UK, more than half of all sales are still in cash.

New 'contactless' technology, though, may mean that we no longer need to carry cash or cards. You simply touch your mobile phone to a reader and the payment is made instantly using a special chip in your phone. It's quicker and cheaper than the card readers we use today, making it economical for even small purchases. In small shops and cafes, customers will spend less time waiting in the queue while people search for the right change. Shoppers in South Korea have already started using the new technology, but how many other countries will it spread to?

Like any new technology, it's likely to take time to spread. Shops will need to install new equipment and users will need to get new phones with the special chips. Experts believe there are more than 380 billion mobile phones in the world and it will take a long time for all those people to change their phones.

Unit 7: Time & Money

Writing
Giving your opinion

Reading

1 Match statements 1-6 about life in the past with statements a–f about modern life.

1 Women spent hours washing clothes by hand. ____
2 Letters took weeks to arrive. ____
3 People made food from the basic ingredients. ____
4 It took a week to go from London to New York. ____
5 People worked on the land from sunrise to sunset. ____
6 People had to collect wood for fires. ____

a We can just switch on the heating.
b We throw everything in the washing machine.
c Emails are sent and received almost instantly.
d It takes 7 hours to travel by plane from London to New York.
e We buy food ready-made from the supermarket.
f Most people work from 9 to 5.

2 Read the two texts below about articles in *The New York Times* from the 19th century. How has life changed since that time? What new inventions have there been?

December 1, 1881

A NEW STEAMSHIP LINE FROM NEW YORK TO LONDON IN LESS THAN SIX DAYS

In December 1881, the New York Times reported on a new company planning to take passengers from New York to London by ship. The ship owner said, 'We propose to build ships which will take a passenger from New York on Monday morning and place him in London before Saturday night. We believe we shall be able to make the trip across in five days, or in five days and a half at most. That may sound strange, but we are confident.'

He explained that Americans are often in a hurry. He said that they value time more than money, so they will pay for a fast service.

Some Needed Inventions
January 8, 1871

An article in January 1871 suggested some possible new inventions. According to the writer, the most needed invention was a machine to wash dishes. He said that women spent too much time with their hands in hot water washing dishes after every meal.

His second hope was for a new kind of lighting. At that time, people used oil lamps to light their homes which were both smelly and dangerous.

---

3 Look at the statistics below. How do people spend their free time around the world now?

- According to a recent survey, an average US citizen watches over 151 hours of television every month. That's around five hours a day.
- TV is the most popular leisure activity in the UK, with the average person watching for 3 hours and 38 minutes a day.
- 83% of American children aged 10–14 spend more than an hour a day on the internet. Many children now spend more time online than watching television.
- 68% of teenagers in the Netherlands spend more than 2 hours a day using a computer.
- On average, an American spends 47 hours a year stuck in traffic jams.
- On 9 May 2008, there were 266 kilometres of queuing traffic in the city of São Paulo in Brazil.
- In Japan, 55% of the population buy a daily newspaper.
- Australia and New Zealand top the list of cinema-going nations. New Zealanders went to the cinema on average 8.1 times each in 2006, Australians made an average of 6.6 visits and Americans 4.8 visits.

Time & Money

Preparing to write

4 Do you agree with the statement below?

We have more free time than ever before, but we spend most of it in front of the television.

Make notes under the following headings. You can add more headings of your own.

Why we have more free time than in the past

- housework and home life
- at work
- transport and communication

How people spend/waste their free time

- television
- computer games
- the internet
- sitting in traffic

5 These sentences giving opinions all have one word missing or one extra word. Can you correct them?

1 It is certainly true that have a lot more free time than our grandparents did.
2 I think it that people could use their free time more wisely.
3 I believe that is important for families to spend time together.
4 We should spend more of our free time for doing exercise and outdoor activities.
5 I don't think that are enough things for young people to do in their free time.

Writing

6 Write an essay giving your opinion about the statements above.

UNIT 8 Home & Away

Grammar 1A
Passive voice

Complete the text with the correct words.

The Welsh village of Llanfairpwllgwyngyllgogerychwyrndrobwllllantysiliogogogoch (1) *is known / is knew* by most local people as Llanfair PG. It (2) *is location / is located* on the island of Anglesey just off the North Wales coast and it (3) *is officially recognised / had officially recognised* as the longest place name in the UK. The village (4) *was originally call / was originally called* Llanfair Pwllgwyngyll, but the name (5) *is changed / was changed* in the 1860s to attract tourists. The village (6) *was connected / were connected* to the mainland in 1826 when the Menai Suspension Bridge (7) *was constructed / constructed* by Thomas Telford. Then in 1850, the Britannia Railway Bridge (8) *builded / was built* and the railway arrived in the village. The long name (9) *was created / is created* by a local man so that when it (10) *was printed / were printed* on the new train timetables people would notice it and be attracted to the area.

Grammar 1B
Passive voice

Complete the second sentence using the passive so that it means the same as the first sentence.

1 British architect, Norman Foster designed Hong Kong International airport.
   Hong Kong airport _____ by British architect, Norman Foster.
2 They built the airport on land reclaimed from the sea.
   The airport _____ on land reclaimed from the sea.
3 They finished the airport in 1998.
   The airport _____ in 1998.
4 Thousands of passengers use the airport every day.
   The airport _____ by thousands of passengers every day.
5 Thousands of tourists visit the Egyptian pyramids every year.
   The Egyptian pyramids _____ by thousands of tourists every year.
6 They used around 2.3 million blocks to build the Great Pyramid at Giza.
   Around 2.3 million blocks _____ to build the Great Pyramid at Giza.
7 People took many valuable objects from inside the pyramids in the early 20th century.
   Many valuable objects _____ from inside the pyramids in the early 20th century.
8 Nowadays, the authorities don't allow tourists to go inside most of the pyramids.
   Nowadays, tourists _____ to go inside most of the pyramids.

Grammar 2
First conditional

Complete the sentences with the correct words.

1 If you have an accident, we *will pay / are pay* your medical costs.
2 If *you'll be / you are* seriously ill or injured, we will fly you home.
3 You can claim up to €1000 if you *lose / lost* your luggage.
4 If your flight *will delayed / is delayed* for more than 12 hours, we will pay for a hotel room.
5 If you need help while abroad, you *can call / will call* our 24-hour helpline.
6 You might not be covered if *you take part / you'll take part* in certain dangerous activities.
7 If *you'll pay / you pay* for 12 months' cover, you will receive a 20% discount.
8 If you want more information, *you can visit / you'll can* visit our website.

Home & Away

Grammar 3A
Second conditional

Match 1–6 with a–f to make conditional sentences.

1 If we had more money, ____
2 The children could each have their own rooms ____
3 If I had the chance, ____
4 If we had a garden, ____
5 The children could play outside more often ____
6 If they lived in the countryside, ____

a they'd have to travel further to school.
b we could have a dog.
c if we moved to a bigger place.
d we'd buy a bigger house.
e if we didn't live in the city centre.
f I'd like to live in the countryside.

Grammar 3B
Second conditional

Complete these sentences with the correct form of the verbs in brackets. Use contractions (*I'd*, etc) where possible.

1 If house prices _____ (*be*) lower, I'd buy my own place.
2 If I owned my own house, I _____ (*paint*) the walls different colours.
3 I'd fix the windows myself if I _____ (*know*) how.
4 We'd move if we _____ (*find*) the right house.
5 If my children wanted to go abroad, I _____ (*not stop*) them.
6 I wouldn't move to a foreign country if I _____ (*not speak*) the language.
7 If I got a job in the city, I _____ (*live*) in the suburbs and commute to work.
8 I _____ (*grow*) my own vegetables if I had a garden.

Grammar 4
Mixed conditionals

Choose the correct sentence *a* or *b*.

1 If the hotel had a website, they'd get more visitors.
   a The hotel already has a website.
   b The hotel hasn't got a website.
2 If the hotel has an internet connection, I'll send you an email.
   a The hotel might have an internet connection.
   b The hotel doesn't have an internet connection.
3 If you stay outside the city centre, it'll be cheaper.
   a The listener is staying in the city centre.
   b The listener hasn't visited the city yet.
4 If you went to Stockholm, you could stay with my brother.
   a The listener is going to Stockholm.
   b The listener hasn't decided where to go yet.
5 I'd fly business class if I could afford it.
   a The speaker sometimes flies business class.
   b The speaker can't afford to fly business class.
6 If it's raining, I'll get a taxi from the station.
   a The speaker is planning to travel by train soon.
   b The speaker is talking about travel generally.

Home & Away

Vocabulary 1
Home

Match the rooms in the box to the pictures.

| bathroom | hall | kitchen | living room |
| bedroom | dining room | | |

1 _____ 2 _____
3 _____ 4 _____
5 _____ 6 _____

Vocabulary 2
Prepositions of movement

Complete the text with the correct words.

Each morning, I go (1) *out of / out from* my front door and turn left. I walk (2) *in / along* the street. I go (3) *past / passed* some shops, then I turn left again (4) *onto / into* a small park. I walk (5) *cross / across* the park. There's a small lake in the middle, so I go (6) *around / out* the edge of the lake. When I get to the other side of the park, I go (7) *across / through* a main road then I take a path that goes (8) *down of / down* the hill to the university at the bottom. I go (9) *through / across* the main gate of the university and (10) *in of / into* the main building. Finally, I walk (11) *up / down* the stairs to my office on the third floor.

Extend your vocabulary 1
Words that mean *trip*

Complete the sentences with the correct words.

1 We went out for a *drive / journey* in the country in his new sports car.
2 We did a *trip / tour* of the city and saw some of the main sights.
3 Did you have a good *trip / ride* to the coast at the weekend?
4 It's only a short taxi *trip / ride* from the airport to the hotel.
5 He goes on regular business *trips / tours* to the US.
6 It was a very long *travel / journey*; a 12-hour *flight / fly* to Nairobi, then a 5-hour bus *trip / ride*.

Home & Away

Vocabulary 3A
Animals

Complete the animal puzzle.

Across

4 a pet with long ears (6)
5 a small pet bird (6)
8 a pet that barks (3)
10 an animal that slides along the ground (5)

Down

1 an animal you can ride (5)
2 an insect with eight legs (6)
3 a small animal with a long tail (5)
6 a pet that lives in water (8)
7 a small pet with soft fur (7)
9 a pet that purrs (3)

Vocabulary 3B
Animals

Complete the words in the sentences.

1 When I was young, I k_____ a hamster as a p_____.
2 I'm afraid of spiders and other insects that have lots of l_____.
3 My daughter's got a rabbit with white f_____ and long e_____.
4 When a dog is happy, it usually wags its t_____.
5 Some people say that dogs often look like their o_____.
6 The disease can affect cats, dogs and other d_____ animals.

Vocabulary 4
Adjectives & prepositions

Complete the texts with a correct preposition in each gap.

I'd like to try snowboarding. I'm quite good (1) _____ skiing, but I'm a bit bored (2) _____ going down the same ski slopes. I'm interested (3) _____ trying something a bit more fun.

We're going on safari to Africa. I'm looking forward to it, but I'm a bit worried (4) _____ some of the animals. I'm afraid (5) _____ snakes and I'm not fond (6) _____ spiders either.

Unit 8 Home & Away

Vocabulary 5
Tourism

Complete the text with the correct words.

(1) *Tourism / Tourist* is an important part of the economy for many Caribbean islands. Traditionally, people (2) *visited / stayed* the Caribbean (3) *for holidays / on holiday* for its tropical beaches. Nowadays, though, ecotourism is becoming more popular with (4) *traveller / travellers*. The small island of Dominica, for example, doesn't have the sandy beaches of other islands, but it is developing its lush green forests as a (5) *touristic place / tourist attraction*. Instead of sun, sea and sand, (6) *tourist activities / tourist's activity* in Dominica are more likely to involve trekking through the rainforest or swimming in waterfalls. The new (7) *tourist / tourists* are more likely to go home with local, organic spices as (8) *souvenirs / memories* than bright t-shirts and sun hats.

Extend your vocabulary 2
house & home

Choose the correct word to complete these sentences.

1. Alicia wasn't feeling well, so she went *house / home* early.
2. My English class is this evening and I haven't done my *housework / homework* yet.
3. They grew up in a huge old *house / home* with a big garden.
4. We painted the outside of the *house / home* white.
5. I called Alex last night, but he wasn't at *house / home*.
6. The small apartment is *house / home* to three adults and four children.
7. I'm going in the same direction, so I'll give you a lift *house / home*.
8. He looks after the children, cooks the meals and does all the *housework / homework*.

Pronunciation 1
/h/

🔊 **1.24** Listen and underline the word in each group that does not contain an /h/ sound.

1 home	hotel	hour
2 house	kitchen	hall
3 haunted	ghost	horror
4 flight	holiday	health
5 historical	unhappy	phone
6 horse	fish	hamster

Pronunciation 2
Conditional sentences

🔊 **1.25** Listen to these sentences and choose the words you hear.

1. If *I could live / I can live* anywhere in the world, *I'll have / I'd have* an apartment in Paris.
2. If you *could change / changed* one thing about your house, what *could you change / would you change*?
3. If we *had / have* children, *we'll probably move / we'd probably move* to a bigger place.
4. *We'll have to / We have to* hire a van if we *moved / move* again.
5. *I'd keep / I'll keep* lots of pets if we *live / lived* in the country.

Listening
Holiday homes

🔊 **1.26** Listen to *Dacha season* and answer these questions.

1. A dacha is …
   a. a public holiday in Russia.
   b. a family home in the countryside.
   c. a holiday home.
2. Traditionally, dachas are …
   a. large apartment blocks.
   b. simple houses.
   c. close to the city.
3. People go to their dacha to …
   a. relax in the countryside and do some gardening.
   b. produce fruit and vegetables for sale.
   c. go walking in the countryside.
4. Many dachas don't have …
   a. gardens.
   b. floors.
   c. modern facilities.
5. The dacha season usually starts …
   a. in the winter.
   b. at the beginning of May.
   c. on 9th May.

Unit 8 Home & Away

Reading
Nomads

1 Read the article *Nomads*. What is a nomad? Which three groups of nomadic people does the article mention?

_____
_____
_____
_____
_____

2 Which of these statements are true for the Mongolians (M), the Sámi (S) and the Bedouin (B)?

	M	S	B
1 They don't live in the same place all the time.			
2 They move to find food for their animals.			
3 They only move a few times a year.			
4 They are mostly herders.			
5 They still live in tents today.			
6 They have legal rights to protect their lifestyle.			

3 Without looking at the article, complete the sentences with passive forms of the verbs in brackets.

1 The ger _____ (*make*) of a round wooden frame.
2 The wooden frame _____ (*cover*) by a heavy felt tent.
3 The ger _____ (*pack*) up.
4 They _____ (*rebuild*) in a new place.
5 The Sámi lifestyle _____ (*threaten*) by changes in the modern world.
6 The right to herd reindeer _____ (*legally protect*).
7 Reindeer herding _____ (*can only do*) by Sámi people.
8 Bedouin tents _____ (*divide*) into two sections by a curtain.

4 Look at this conditional sentence about the Sámi. Complete the conditional sentence about the Bedouin.

If the Sámi can't move their herds to their feeding areas, their lifestyle will disappear.

If the Bedouin _____ their animals regularly, they _____ enough food and water.

Nomads

For most people, home is a fixed place; a house or a flat in a town or a village. But for some groups of people around the world, home is not fixed. Nomadic people move from place to place, often following the animals which they herd or hunt.

The nomadic hunters of **Mongolia** live in large tents called *ger*. The ger are made of a round wooden frame which is covered by a heavy tent. It has one room where the whole family sleeps, cooks and eats. Groups of families move at least twice a year from a summer to a winter camp. The ger are packed up and rebuilt in a new place.

The **Sámi** people live in the northern part of Norway, Finland and Sweden. Traditionally, many Sámi are reindeer herders and in the past, whole families moved with the reindeer herds, living in tents. Nowadays most Sámi families live in towns or villages, but the herders still move with their animals. Like many nomadic groups, their lifestyle is threatened by changes in the modern world. If the Sámi can't move their herds to their feeding areas, their lifestyle will disappear. In Norway, the right to herd reindeer is legally protected and can only be done by Sámi people.

The **Bedouin** people live in the deserts of Arabia and north-east Africa. They are nomadic herders who travel through the desert by camel with their sheep and goats. Because the land is so hot and dry, they have to move often to find enough food and water for their animals. They live in simple tents which are divided into two sections by a curtain. One part is for men and for guests. The other part is where the women live and cook.

Glossary
herd (*noun*) a large group of animals of the same type that move about together
herd (*verb*) to make a group of animals move together to another place
herder (*noun*) someone who looks after a herd of animals and moves them from place to place
nomad (*noun*) someone who belongs to a group of people who move from place to place
nomadic (*adjective*) moving from place to place

Unit 8 Home & Away

Writing
Describing a place

Reading

1 Read the two texts below about Barcelona. Which one is from a guidebook and which one was written by a visitor?

24-hours in Barcelona

1

Last year, I visited Barcelona for a conference. I stayed at a hotel in the north of the city, near the conference centre and I didn't have much time for sightseeing. I just had one day after the conference to explore the city. I started on the waterfront with a cup of coffee in the sunshine. Then I walked slowly up the famous *Ramblas*, a wide avenue with shops and cafés. It had a great atmosphere, buzzing with people. At the end of the afternoon, I got to the *Passeig de Gracia* to see some of the fantastic buildings which were designed by Antoni Gaudí. It's an amazing city and there's so much to see. If I go back again, I'll definitely visit the *Sagrada Familia* and some of the museums.

2

Start your day at one of Barcelona's most famous landmarks, the *Sagrada Familia*. This amazing cathedral was designed by Antoni Gaudí. Building work started in 1882 and it hasn't been finished yet! It's now a popular tourist attraction, so arrive early to avoid the crowds. If the queues aren't too long, you could climb one of the towers to see the mixture of architectural styles close up. For lunch, stroll down the *Ramblas* and stop at one of the many cafés. Most cafés serve delicious tapas; small plates of Spanish food. Then, in the afternoon, head for the beach. At *Platja Barceloneta* you'll find the *Club de Natació Atlètic Barceloneta*. It opened in 1913 and it has an open-air pool, sauna and gym. At the end of a hard day's sightseeing, it's a great place to relax.

Language focus

2 Match sentences 1–7 with the grammatical features a–g.

1 I stayed at a hotel in the north of the city. _____
2 There's so much to see. _____
3 If I go back again, I'll definitely visit _____
4 Building work was started in 1882. _____
5 It hasn't been finished yet. _____
6 Most cafés serve delicious tapas. _____
7 It has an open-air swimming pool. _____

a *there* – something mentioned for the first time
b passive voice to focus on the action
c past simple for a past experience
d present simple for general facts
e *it* – something already mentioned
f present perfect – something hasn't happened yet
g first conditional

Vocabulary

3 Find words in the texts to match these definitions.

1 the activity of travelling around a place to see the interesting things _____
2 to travel around a place to learn more about it _____
3 the mood or feeling that exists in a place _____
4 with a lot of noise or activity _____
5 a famous building that you can see and recognise easily _____
6 a place to visit that is very popular with tourists _____
7 to walk without hurrying _____

Preparing to write

4 Think about a place you have visited as a tourist. Write some notes to answer the questions below.

- When did you go there?
- Where did you stay?
- Did you go sightseeing?
- What are the main landmarks and tourist attractions?
- Why did you like the place? (architecture, food, atmosphere, landscape, activities, etc.)

Writing

5 One of your friends is planning to go to a place that you have already visited. Write an email describing your visit and the main attractions.

UNIT 9 Health & Fitness

Grammar 1A
Modal verbs of advice

Decide if the sentences are correct or incorrect.

Grandmother's advice

1 You shouldn't going out with wet hair.
   You'll catch a cold.   Correct / Incorrect
2 You should always drink water with
   a meal.   Correct / Incorrect
3 You ought eat fish before your
   exams. It's good for the brain.   Correct / Incorrect
4 You mustn't to go swimming for
   an hour after you've eaten.   Correct / Incorrect
5 Children shouldn't drink coffee.
   It stops them growing.   Correct / Incorrect
6 You should eat more carrots.
   They'll help you see in the dark.   Correct / Incorrect
7 You must always to read in good
   light or you'll damage your eyes.   Correct / Incorrect

Grammar 1B
Modal verbs of advice

Complete the second sentence so that it has the same meaning as the first sentence. Use the words in brackets.

Advice for long flights

- If you're on a long flight, it's important to get up regularly and walk around.

  On long flights, you (1) _____ regularly and walk around. (*should*)

- Drink plenty of water, but avoid alcohol and caffeine.

  You (2) _____ plenty of water, but you (3) _____ alcohol or caffeine. (*should / shouldn't*)

- If you're on regular medication, make sure you take enough for the whole journey and extra in case of delays.

  You (4) _____ enough medication for the whole journey and extra in case of delays. (*must*)

- If you usually wear contact lenses, it's best to take your glasses in case you want to sleep.

  Contact lens wearers (5) _____ their glasses in case they want to sleep. (*ought to*)

- Don't wear tight clothing, choose something loose and comfortable.

  You (6) _____ tight clothing, you (7) _____ something loose and comfortable. (*shouldn't / should*)

- On night flights, it helps if you try to sleep for at least some of the time.

  You (8) _____ to sleep for at least some of the time on night flights. (*ought to*)

Grammar 2

Complete the text with the correct verb forms.

Before the invention of refrigeration, people (1) *couldn't keep / couldn't kept* fresh food for very long before it went bad. Dairy products, like milk, (2) *had be used / had to be used* within a few days. Different methods were developed to help store food. Fresh meat was often dried so that people (3) *could to keep / could keep* it for longer. Traditionally, fish was salted or smoked so that people (4) *didn't have to eat / hadn't to eat* it straight away. Fruit growers (5) *can stored / could store* their fruit for a few weeks in a cool place, but to keep it for longer, they (6) *had to cooked / had to cook* it in sugar to make jam.

Grammar 3A
Past perfect

Complete this text with the past perfect forms of the verbs in brackets. Use contractions (*he'd*, etc) where possible.

Last week, I emailed some friends to try to organise a game of football on Saturday. Tim couldn't come because he (1) _____ (*injure*) his ankle on a skiing holiday the week before. Michael said he couldn't play because he (2) _____ (*hurt*) his knee. Apparently, he (3) _____ (*trip*) over the cat! Ryan had food poisoning after he (4) _____ (*eat*) some bad food. Maurizio couldn't make it because his car (5) _____ (*break*) down and he (6) _____ (*take*) it to the garage. Theo said no, because he (7) _____ (*already / promise*) to take his girlfriend away for the weekend. And James didn't even get my message because his computer (8) _____ (*crash*).

Unit 9 Health & Fitness

Grammar 3B
Past perfect

Underline the event which happened first.

1. Tim couldn't go because he'd injured his leg.
2. Michael had hurt his knee so he couldn't play.
3. Ryan had food poisoning because he'd eaten some bad food.
4. Maurizio took his car to the garage because it had broken down.
5. Theo had promised to take his girlfriend away, so he said no.
6. James didn't get the message because his computer had crashed.

Grammar 4
Reported statements

Complete the reported statements.

1. 'The team played really well.'
   The manager said that _____ really well.
2. 'I've trained hard and I'm confident of doing well.'
   In an interview before the race, she said _____ hard and _____ confident of doing well.
3. 'I'm really disappointed that we didn't win.'
   He told reporters _____ really disappointed that _____.
4. 'Anderson isn't playing because he's injured his shoulder.'
   The coach said that Anderson _____ because _____ his shoulder.
5. 'It definitely wasn't a penalty!'
   An angry fan complained that _____ a penalty.

Vocabulary 1
Feeling ill

Complete the conversations with the correct word.

A: What's (1) *the matter / the wrong*? You don't look very well.
B: I think I've (2) *caught / taken* a cold. I've got a (3) *pain / sore* throat and a (4) *blocked / wet* nose.
C: I don't feel very (5) *fine / well*.
D: Oh dear, what's (6) *bad / wrong*?
C: (7) *I feel / I've got* a terrible headache and (8) *I feel / I've got* sick.

Vocabulary 2
Medical treatment

Complete the texts with the verbs in the box.

| break | cause | consult | go | have |
| stay | take | visit | | |

Some patients who (1) _____ a bone just have it put in plaster. Others have to (2) _____ an operation and (3) _____ in hospital for several days or even weeks.

To keep your teeth healthy, you should (4) _____ the dentist regularly. We recommend that you (5) _____ for a check-up every six months.

You should (6) _____ no more than 8 tablets in 24 hours. The tablets may (7) _____ drowsiness. If your symptoms continue, you should (8) _____ a doctor.

Vocabulary 3
Medicine

Match 1–7 and a–f to make sentences.

1. Before anaesthesia
2. There are now vaccines
3. Improved sanitation
4. Antibiotics are used
5. A thermometer is used
6. Bacteria can only be seen

a. can stop the spread of disease.
b. under a microscope.
c. patients were awake during operations.
d. to treat infections.
e. to prevent many common diseases.
f. to check a patient's temperature.

Health & Fitness

Vocabulary 4
Sports

Complete the sentences with *do*, *go*, or *play*.

1 People usually _____ skiing in the winter.
2 People of all ages _____ swimming in pools or in the sea.
3 You can _____ tennis with either two or four people.
4 People often _____ yoga to relax and keep their body loose.
5 Some people _____ cycling for pleasure, others as a way of getting around.
6 People usually _____ aerobics as part of a class.
7 You can _____ volleyball on a court or on the beach.
8 Many older people _____ golf as it's a very gentle form of exercise.
9 Young boys around the world _____ football in parks and in the street.
10 When people _____ judo, they wear a white uniform called a judogi.

Vocabulary 5
Sport

Complete the text with the correct words.

Most schoolchildren take part in sports or some kind of physical education, but what is the value of sport in the school timetable? Some people argue that playing (1) *team / group* sports like football or volleyball teaches children to work together with the other (2) *athletes / players*. Some people think children should take part in (3) *single / individual* sports like running because being a (4) *winner / win* gives them self-confidence. On the other hand, for every child who wins a (5) *run / race*, there will be many more (6) *loosers / losers*. Others say that physical exercise is important for children's health, so it doesn't really matter whether they (7) *play / make* basketball, (8) *do / go* swimming or even (9) *do / take* aerobics, the health benefits are the same.

Extend your vocabulary
win and *beat*

Complete the sentences with the correct verb.

1 Uruguay *beat / won* the first Football World Cup in 1930. They *beat / won* Argentina 4–2 in the final.
2 In the final of the first Cricket World Cup in 1975, the West Indies *beat / won* Australia by 17 runs.
3 The first tennis competition at Wimbledon *was beaten / was won* by Spencer Gore in 1877.
4 At the first modern Olympic Games in 1896, the United States *beat / won* the most gold medals, with Greece *beating / winning* the most medals in total (gold, silver and bronze).
5 American, Tom Burke *beat / won* the first Olympic 100 metres final, *beating / winning* German, Fritz Hoffmann by 0.2 seconds.

Vocabulary 6
Say, tell, and *ask*

Complete the sentences with the correct form of *ask*, *say* or *tell*.

1 When fans _____ you for your autograph, it's difficult to _____ no.
2 The manager usually _____ us who will be in the team a few days before a match.
3 Reporters always _____ questions about your private life.
4 Last week, a TV interviewer _____ me about my children, but I _____ him I wouldn't talk about my family.
5 Some people _____ that sportspeople are paid too much, but we only have a very short career.

Unit 9 Health & Fitness

Pronunciation 1
ch and gh

🔊 **1.27** Listen to the sentences. Are the underlined sounds the same or different?

1 I've got a hea<u>dache</u> and a terrible cou<u>gh</u>. *Same / Different*
2 He didn't go to <u>sch</u>ool because he had a stoma<u>ch</u> a<u>ch</u>e. *Same / Different*
3 If you ca<u>tch</u> a cold you ou<u>gh</u>t to drink plenty of water. *Same / Different*
4 You have to <u>ch</u>oose the right team for ea<u>ch</u> ma<u>tch</u>. *Same / Different*
5 There's a special te<u>ch</u>nique for using the rowing ma<u>ch</u>ine. *Same / Different*
6 The race will be tou<u>gh</u> if you don't do enou<u>gh</u> training. *Same / Different*

Pronunciation 2
Word stress

🔊 **1.28** Listen and underline the word with a different stress pattern.

1 medical   pharmacy   injection   hospital
2 operation ambulance   preservation sanitation
3 prescription translation infection medicine
4 disease   doctor   symptom   treatment
5 tournament marathon   individual   stadium

Listening
How much exercise is good for you?

🔊 **1.29** Listen to an interview about exercise and complete the sentences with the correct word.

1 You ought to do around *thirty / forty* minutes of exercise five times a week.
2 Thirty minutes of exercise three times a week still has some *health / healthy* benefits.
3 You should do some exercise that raises your heart rate, such as *walking / running*.
4 If you exercise *regularly / effectively*, you can reduce your risk of many illnesses.
5 Employees who exercise at work are *healthier / happier* and more productive.
6 Men in their fifties who exercise regularly live longer than men who *do / make* no exercise at all.

Reading
Heart transplant surgery

1 Read the article *A second life* and answer the questions.

1 Who did the first human heart transplant operation?
_____
_____

2 When was the operation?
_____
_____
_____

3 Where was the operation?
_____
_____

4 How long did the operation take?
_____
_____

5 How long did the patient live after the operation?
_____
_____

2 A quotation is the exact words of someone else that you use in a piece of writing. Quotations are usually written inside quotation marks (" "). Look at the quotation from Christiaan Barnard in the article. Which of these best represents his idea?

a If someone is being chased by a lion, they will do anything to escape.
b If someone is very ill, they will decide to have a transplant operation because it will save their life.
c If someone is dying, they will choose a dangerous operation because if they don't, they will die anyway.

3 Look at the words from the article. Are they people (P), medical conditions (MC) or medical treatment (MT)?

1 transplant operation   _____
2 surgeon   _____
3 operation   _____
4 donor   _____
5 medical team   _____
6 patient   _____
7 pneumonia   _____

Health & Fitness

4 Look at the sentences from the article. Which event happened first? Which verb tense is used to show this?

1 Before he *performed* the operation, Dr Barnard *had spent* many years doing similar operations on animals.
2 The new heart *came* from a woman who *had died* in a road accident.
3 Barnard *continued* to perform transplant operations after other surgeons *had given up*.

5 Complete the sentences using the past perfect of the verb in brackets. Use contractions where possible.

1 Surgeons _____ (*already / perform*) successful kidney transplants when the first heart transplant operation took place.
2 Christiaan Barnard retired as a surgeon in 1983 because he _____ (*develop*) arthritis in his hands.
3 In 2001, Kelly Perkins climbed Mount Kilimanjaro in Tanzania, six years after she _____ (*have*) a heart transplant.
4 In 2008, Canadian Dwight Kroening completed an Ironman race, a 2.4-mile swim, a 112-mile bike ride and a 26.2-mile run, 22 years after he _____ (*receive*) a donor heart.

A second life

The first human heart transplant operation was performed by surgeon Christiaan Barnard in South Africa in 1967. Before he performed the operation, Dr Barnard had spent many years doing similar operations on animals. For the first human transplant, the donor heart came from a woman who had died in a road accident. The operation lasted nine hours and involved a medical team of thirty people. The patient only lived for 18 days before dying of pneumonia. Many years later, Barnard wrote about his decision to carry out that first heart transplant.

"For a dying man it is not a difficult decision because he knows he is at the end. If a lion chases you to the bank of a river filled with crocodiles, you will leap into the water convinced you have a chance to swim to the other side. But you would not accept such odds if there were no lion."

Christiaan Barnard

Many early heart transplant patients only lived for a few days or weeks. However, Barnard continued to perform transplant operations and to develop new techniques after other surgeons had given up. Eventually, the success of the operations improved and there are now people alive who had heart transplants more than 30 years ago. Nowadays, more than 85% of heart transplant patients live for a year or more and around 70% of patients live for more than five years after the operation.

Barnard died in 2001 at the age of 78.

Glossary

surgeon (*noun*) – a doctor who performs operations
donor (*noun*) – someone who gives something such as blood or part of their body to help someone else
patient (*noun*) – someone who is receiving medical treatment
perform (*verb*) – to complete an action or activity
pneumonia (*noun*) – a serious illness that affects your lungs
transplant (*noun*) – a medical operation in which a new organ is put into a person's body

Unit 9 Health & Fitness

Writing
Giving advice

Reading

1 Read the advice below for first-time skiers.

If you're going on your first ski trip, here are a few tips:

Before you go …

Make sure you're going to a resort that's good for beginners. It should have nursery slopes and plenty of easy runs. The easiest slopes are usually called blue runs.

You don't need to buy a lot of expensive equipment, but you should get some ski pants, a ski jacket and a good pair of gloves. If you don't want to buy them, try asking friends. They may have things you can borrow.

Before you go skiing, you ought to do some exercises to prepare yourself. There are plenty of good websites with simple ski exercises.

When you arrive …

You must get a comfortable pair of boots, so it's worth spending plenty of time at the ski hire shop. Don't be afraid to try on lots of different pairs.

If you're a complete beginner, you should probably start with some lessons. Group lessons are usually cheaper and it's more fun to learn with other people.

Beginners always fall over a lot, so don't get disappointed. If you try to do too much in the first few days, you'll just get really tired. So take it gently. For example, you could just have lessons in the morning and then relax in the afternoon for the first couple of days.

Language focus: giving advice

2 Complete the sentences from the text which give advice.

1 _____ you're going to a resort that's good for beginners.
2 _____ a lot of expensive equipment.
3 _____ some ski pants, a ski jacket and a good pair of gloves.
4 If you don't want to buy them, _____ friends.
5 Before you go skiing, _____ some exercises.
6 _____ a comfortable pair of boots.
7 _____ plenty of time at the ski hire shop.
8 _____ try on lots of different pairs.
9 _____ lessons in the morning.

Vocabulary

3 Add more ideas to the table of clothing and equipment needed for these sports.

Skiing	Tennis	Cycling	Golf
skis	tennis racket	cycling shorts	golf shoes
ski boots			
ski poles			
ski pants			
jacket			
gloves			

Health & Fitness

Writing

4 Read these emails asking for advice.

Hi,

With the summer coming up, I'm thinking of taking up tennis. I've never played before, but we've got public tennis courts in a park near the house. You play tennis, don't you? Any advice? Do I need to get an expensive racket? What about lessons?

Thanks!

Hello,

We've just booked a holiday in the countryside. We'll probably do some walking, but we'd like to go cycling too. You cycle quite a bit, don't you? Is there anything you think we should consider? We'll probably hire bikes, but is there any other equipment we need? Any advice welcome!

Thanks!

Hi!

My new job's going really well and I'm getting on well with my colleagues. Quite a few of them play golf at the weekends. I'd like to join them, but I don't know anything about golf. Do you still play? Got any advice? Do you think I need to buy my own golf clubs? And what do I need to wear? I don't want to turn up wearing the wrong thing!

Thanks!

Imagine that one of these emails is from a friend of yours. Write an email reply giving some advice.

You could write about:

- equipment
- clothing
- lessons
- fitness
- where to go

UNIT 10 New & Old

Grammar 1A
Defining relative clauses

Complete the text with the correct relative pronouns.

In the past, people (1) *who / which* didn't have access to telephones used to send urgent messages by telegram. A telegram was a short message (2) *who / which* was sent over long distances using a telegraph machine. The sender wrote down the message (3) *who / that* they wanted to send and took it to their local post office. There, the telegraph operator sent it using a special code. At the other end, there was another telegraph operator (4) *who / which* wrote the message down on a piece of paper (5) *who / which* was then delivered by hand to the recipient.

Nowadays, we have lots of different ways of contacting people quickly. Text messages, or SMS, are short written messages (6) *who /that* you send from your mobile phone. Real-time communication is communication (7) *who / which* happens very quickly, so the person (8) *which / who* you contact can reply straight away. Instant messaging is a system of real-time communication (9) *who / which* uses the internet to let you *chat* to another computer user (10) *who / which* is online in a kind of written conversation.

Grammar 1B
Defining relative clauses

Complete the definitions with a relative clause using *which* or *who*.

1 A 'newcomer' is a person. The person has recently started to live or work somewhere.
 A 'newcomer' is a person _____ to live or work somewhere.
2 A 'newborn' is a baby. The baby has just been born.
 A 'newborn' is a baby _____ born.
3 The 'New World' is the American continent. It was first visited by Europeans in the 16th century.
 The 'New World' is the American continent _____ by Europeans in the 16th century.
4 A 'New Year's resolution' is a decision about things you will do or avoid. You make it on the first day of the year.
 A 'New Year's resolution' is a decision _____ on the first day of the year about things you will do or avoid.
5 An 'old banger' is a car. It is old and doesn't work very well.
 An 'old banger' is a car _____ and doesn't work very well.
6 An 'old hand' is a person. The person has been doing something for a long time and is good at it.
 An 'old hand' is a person _____ something for a long time and is good at it.
7 An 'old wives' tale' is a traditional belief. Many people think it is wrong or silly.
 An 'old wives' tale' is a traditional belief _____ wrong or silly.

Unit 10 New & Old

Grammar 2A
Definite article (the)

Why is a definite article (the) used in these sentences? Write a, b, c or d next to each sentence.

a there is only one person or thing
b the person or thing has been referred to before
c it's part of a name
d it's part of a superlative

1 My new mobile didn't work, so I took the phone back to the shop. ____
2 People get a lot of news from the internet. ____
3 Google is one of the most popular internet search engines. ____
4 New insects are still being discovered in the Amazon rainforest. ____
5 New Caledonia is an island in the Pacific. ____
6 Scientists believe the world is around 4.5 billion years old. ____
7 The oldest tree ever known was around 5,000 years old. ____
8 Her elderly neighbour doesn't have any family, so she visits the old lady regularly. ____

Grammar 2B
Definite article (the)

Complete the text with *the*, *a* or no article (–).

In 1964, (1) *a / the* researcher got permission from (2) *– / the* United States Forest Service to cut down (3) *the / a* bristlecone pine tree in (4) *the / a* Great Basin National Park. (5) *The / A* park is in (6) *the / –* Nevada in (7) *– / the* west of (8) *– / the* US and contains many very old trees. (9) *The / –* researcher wanted to study (10) *the / a* rings inside these ancient trees. When he counted (11) *the / a* rings inside (12) *a / the* tree he had cut down, he found that there were around 4,900 growth rings. This meant it was almost 5,000 years old, (13) *an / the* oldest known tree.

Unit 10 New & Old

Grammar 3
Verb form review

Match the sentences 1–8 with the verb forms a–h.

1. Every year, thousands of tourists visit Stonehenge.
2. The circle of stones was built more than 4,000 years ago.
3. According to experts, people first made a circle of 80 stones.
4. The stones had been brought from Wales, 250 kilometres away.
5. Later, people added a smaller circle with stones resting on the top.
6. Stonehenge has been a UNESCO World Heritage site since 1986.
7. If you visit Stonehenge, you won't be able to walk among the stones.
8. You can only look at the stones from behind a fence.

a irregular past simple
b real conditional
c regular past simple
d present simple
e past perfect
f modal verb
g present perfect
h past simple passive

Grammar 4
Both, neither

Complete the text with the correct words.

Cordoba is a city in southern Spain. It is also the name of a city in Central Argentina. The people in (1) *both cities / both of city* speak Spanish. (2) *Both city has / Both cities have* beautiful churches and historical monuments that are popular with tourists. (3) *Both place is / Both places are* inland, (4) *neither of them / neither of places* is on the coast.

The Australian city of Newcastle was founded at the beginning of the 19th century and was named after the city of Newcastle upon Tyne in the North of England. The two cities have many things in common. (5) *Both of them are / Both of them is* in coal-mining areas and (6) *both is / both are* important ports. And of course, the people in (7) *both of places / both places* speak English.

London is the capital of the United Kingdom, but it's also the name of a large city in Canada. The two cities (8) *both have / both has* rivers with the same name; the Thames. In terms of climate, (9) *both city is / both cities are* cold in the winter and warm in the summer, although the Canadian London has much colder winters.
(10) *Neither city is / Neither cities are* as hot as another London; the capital of the tiny island of Kiritimati in the Pacific Ocean.

UNIT 10 New & Old

Vocabulary 1
New words in context

Complete the descriptions with words from the box.

| carbon | blog | brunch | email | mouse | virus |

1 A computer _____ got its name because it looks a little like the animal with its long tail.
2 When we eat _____ it's a meal that combines breakfast and lunch.
3 Your footprint is a mark you leave on the ground, so your _____ footprint is the mark you leave on the planet.
4 A log is a type of diary you keep, so a _____, short for a web log, is a kind of online diary.
5 We now talk about a computer _____ because it's similar to a disease that spreads between people.
6 The e- in new words like _____ and ebanking is short for electronic.

Vocabulary 2A
Places

Match the descriptions 1–7 to the place names a–g.

1 capital   a China
2 city   b Earth
3 country   c Toronto
4 continent   d Cuba
5 planet   e Florida
6 state   f Paris
7 island   g Europe

Vocabulary 2B
Places

Complete the words in the texts.

Although Sydney, in the (1) s_____ of New South Wales, is the biggest (2) c_____ in Australia, with a population of over 4 million, Canberra is actually the (3) c_____ of the (4) c_____.

The tiny English (5) v_____ of Woolstrope-by-Colsterworth is famous as the (6) b_____ of the scientist Sir Isaac Newton.

Extend your vocabulary 1
Words that mean *new*

Complete the sentences with the correct words.

1 Scientists are using *cutting-edge / biting-edge* technology to explore the ocean floor.
2 His *latest / later* book is about a female detective in Mumbai, India.
3 The jacket was *fresh / brand* new, I'd only bought it the week before.
4 The new manager has introduced some very *innovative / recent* ideas which have changed the way we work.
5 The engines of many *dated / modern* cars are controlled by computer technology.
6 Nothing we've tried so far has worked. We need a *fresh / clean* approach to the problem.

Unit 10 75

Unit 10 New & Old

Vocabulary 3A
Transport

Write the form of transport under the pictures.

1 _____
2 _____
3 _____
4 _____
5 _____
6 _____

Vocabulary 3B
Transport

Choose the correct answers.

1 Which form of transport doesn't have wheels?
   a bicycle
   b ship
   c bus
2 Which form of transport has wings?
   a underground
   b plane
   c boat
3 Where do you catch a train?
   a stop
   b track
   c station
4 Which form of transport doesn't have an engine?
   a bicycle
   b motorbike
   c car
5 Which form of transport has a driver?
   a bicycle
   b plane
   c taxi
6 Which form of transport doesn't run on tracks?
   a underground
   b train
   c bus

Vocabulary 4
Transport verbs

Complete the texts with the correct words.

Commuting around the world.

Around the world, more and more people are (1) *getting to / getting on* their bicycles and cycling to work. In New York, for example, the number of people who (2) *drove / rode* to work increased by 35% from 2007 to 2008. Beijing, however, is really the city of bicycles, with more than 10 million bikes. An estimated 38% of Beijingers travel (3) *by bicycle / on bike* every day. However, cars are quickly replacing bikes, with around 3.3 million cars (4) *running / driving* around the city's streets in 2008.

The US city with the most taxis per capita is Bethel in Alaska. With no roads going in or out of this remote city, there are almost no private cars. To get to Bethel, you have to (5) *get in / get on* a plane or a boat. But if residents want to get across the city, they (6) *get in / get on* a taxi and (7) *get off / get out* on the other side of town.

Unit 10 New & Old

Extend your vocabulary 2
Words that mean *make*

Complete the sentences with words in the box.

| built causing designed developing |
| manufacture produced |

1 For many European companies, it's cheaper to _____ goods in Asia.
2 In 2007, Japan _____ more cars than any other country in the world.
3 Many modern cars are _____ to use less fuel.
4 As the price of oil rises, car makers are _____ cars which run on other forms of fuel.
5 Scientists think that global warming is already _____ changes to our climate.
6 The Shea Stadium, home of the New York Mets baseball team, was _____ in 1964 and demolished in 2008 to make way for a car park.

Vocabulary 5
Games

Complete the sentences with the correct words.

Trivial Pursuit

Each (1) *gamer / player* has a (2) *counter / marker* which they move around the (3) *table / board*. When it's your (4) *next / turn* you (5) *roll the dice / turn the pieces* and move that number of places. Each (6) *square / space* is a different colour and each colour represents a different topic. For example, if you (7) *fall in / land on* yellow, you have to answer a question about history or green prompts a question about science and nature. If you answer correctly, you (8) *earn / win* a coloured (9) *piece / plastic*. The object is to collect all six colours.

Pronunciation 1
Consonant clusters

🔊 1.30 Listen to the phrases and tick (✔) the sound you hear.

	/pl/	/tr/	/st/	/str/
1				
2				
3				
4				
5				

	/pl/	/tr/	/st/	/str/
6				
7				
8				
9				
10				

Pronunciation 2
Sentence stress

🔊 1.31 Listen to these sentences and choose the stress pattern you hear, <u>a</u> or <u>b</u>.

1 a To <u>start</u> the <u>game</u>, you <u>roll</u> the <u>dice</u>.
  b To start <u>the game</u>, you roll <u>the dice</u>.
2 a You go <u>down</u> the <u>snakes</u> and <u>up</u> the <u>ladders</u>.
  b <u>You go</u> down the <u>snakes</u> and up the <u>ladders</u>.
3 a If <u>you throw</u> a <u>six</u>, <u>you miss</u> a turn.
  b If <u>you</u> <u>throw</u> a <u>six</u>, you <u>miss</u> a <u>turn</u>.
4 a I really <u>have</u> to go <u>now</u>.
  b I <u>really</u> have to <u>go</u> now.
5 a It's getting <u>late</u>. I'd <u>better</u> be <u>going</u>.
  b It's <u>getting</u> late. <u>I'd better</u> be going.

Listening
The oldest

1 🔊 1.32 Listen to people talking about some very old things. What four things do they talk about?

1 a _____
2 a _____
3 a _____
4 a _____

2 🔊 1.32 Listen again and choose the correct options to complete the information in the table.

The world's oldest …	Age	Location
city	(1) *10,000 years / 1,000 years*	Syria
(2) *working clock / church clock*	600 years +	(3) *Italy / England*
(4) *holy text / printed book*	(5) *1,000 years + / 100 years +*	China
University	1,000 years +	(6) *Egypt and Morocco / Egypt and Italy*

Unit 10 New & Old

Reading

Before you read

1 Answer these questions.

1 Where do you look for information for your work or studies? Be specific.

2 Have you ever used an encyclopedia on CD-ROM? What was its name?

3 Do you have a printed encyclopedia? If not, did your parents or grandparents have one?

2 Match the dates with the events in the history of encyclopedias.

1 The 4th century BC ____
2 80 AD ____
3 220 ____
4 The 16th century ____
5 The 1980s ____
6 2001 ____

a The word *encyclopedia* was used for a book for the first time.
b The online encyclopedia *Wikipedia* started.
c Some experts think the first encyclopedia was produced.
d The first encyclopedias on CD-ROM were produced.
e The oldest encyclopedia that exists today was published.
f The first Chinese encyclopedia was written.

3 Read the article *Encyclopedias past and present* and check your answers to exercise 2.

4 Correct the sentences.

1 The word *encyclopedia* comes from a Greek word.

2 A few copies of the *Disciplinae* exist today.

3 The first encyclopedias were reference books for students.

4 Information on the first digital encyclopedias was organised alphabetically.

5 The first encyclopedia on CD-ROM only had text.

6 *Historia Naturalis* is the world's biggest encyclopedia.

5 Complete the definitions with a relative pronoun. Then find words in the article to match the definitions.

1 A thing _____ gives us something we need. (Paragraph 1)
_____

2 Information about the world _____ many people know. (Paragraph 1)
_____

3 A person _____ studies history. (Paragraph 3)
_____

4 A person _____ started something new. (Paragraph 3)
_____

5 One book _____ is part of a collection of books. (Paragraph 5)
_____

6 The words in a text _____ tell you what the text is about. (Paragraph 6)
_____

6 Find the first example in the article of these forms.

1 a regular present simple verb

2 an irregular past simple verb

3 a present perfect verb form

4 a past passive verb form

Unit 10 New & Old

5   a present passive verb form
_____
_____

6   a relative clause
_____
_____

7   an infinitive of purpose
_____
_____

Encyclopedias past and present

The Internet has revolutionised the way that we look for information. It's hard to imagine that just three decades ago, printed encyclopedias were our main source of general knowledge. But the Internet is relatively new, and printed encyclopedias have a two-thousand year history.

The word *encyclopedia* comes from an Ancient Greek phrase pronounced 'enkyklios paideia' which means 'complete system of learning', or 'comprehensive education'. Later, it was written incorrectly as one word and it was first used to describe an encyclopedia in Germany in the 16th century.

Some historians think the encyclopedia has Greek origins too. The Greek philosopher Aristotle (384-322 BC) wrote about many subjects and is sometimes called the father of encyclopedias. It is also possible that an encyclopedia was produced in Greece in the 4th century BC, but no copy has survived. No copy of an encyclopedia called *Disciplinae* (the Disciplines) has survived either, but historians know that this encyclopedia was produced in Rome in 30 BC. The oldest encyclopedia that still exists today was published in Rome in 80 AD. It's called *Historia Naturalis* (Natural History), consists of 37 volumes, and is still consulted today for information about the Roman world.

Encyclopedias developed in other parts of the world too. Historians know that an encyclopedia called *Huanglan* (The Emperor's Mirror) was written in China in about the year 220, and an encyclopedia was written in Basra in Iraq in about 960.

Although some of these early encyclopedias looked like a modern printed encyclopedia, they were used in a very different way. Today's encyclopedias are reference works that you consult when you need information. Early encyclopedias had volumes on different subjects and were used in a similar way to textbooks today.

The modern encyclopedia was developed in the 18th century, when it became popular to organise information alphabetically and have short entries. This format was popular until the first digital versions appeared on CD-ROM in the mid 1980s. Information on these encyclopedias was organised by subject, but you could access it in different ways – alphabetically, by subject, by key words and by clicking on hyperlinks. Entries included audio and video material too.

However, encyclopedias on CD-ROM didn't survive for very long. It became clear that the internet was the ideal place for an encyclopedia because you can update information constantly. The online encyclopedia *Wikipedia* was started in 2001 and has become the largest and most extensive encyclopedia ever compiled.

> **Glossary**
> **BC** (*adverb*) – abbreviation for 'before Christ' to indicate dates before the system of years we use today
> **AD** (*adverb*) – an abbreviation that indicates a date after the birth of Christ
> **entry** (*noun*) – a text about one subject in an encyclopedia
> **update** (*verb*) – to add the most recent information about something

Unit 10 New & Old

Writing
A report on a new facility

Reading

1 Read the report that a student has written. What is the report about? What is the missing word?

> **A**
>
> I went to visit the town's new public _____ this week, and would like to tell the rest of the class about it. It's located in a new building in the High Street and replaces the old _____, which was in a converted church in Green Lane, next to the railway station.
>
> **B**
>
> My impression of the new _____ was very positive. Because it's in the centre, a lot more people will see it and use it. Also, it has disabled access, and that's something that the old _____ didn't have. What's more, the _____ uses all the latest technology. There's free internet access for anyone in the cafe for up to 30 minutes, and members can use the internet for free at the _____'s other computers. And borrowing a book is now computerised.
>
> **C**
>
> However, there are some things I preferred about the old building. As I'm not fond of modern architecture, I think the new building is less interesting, and I loved the old church. Also, the new _____ was very busy. I had to wait for 20 minutes to borrow a book, and all the computers were busy.
>
> **D**
>
> But overall, I think the new _____ is a great improvement on the old one, and it makes the town a better, more modern place to live in.

2 Read the report again and tick (✔) the things it mentions about the new facility.

Where it is

Access for people in wheelchairs

The architecture

How to become a member

Modern technology

Language focus: organising a report

3 Which paragraph in the report ...

1 gives the writer's conclusion? _____
2 talks about positive things? _____
3 introduces the subject of the report? _____
4 talks about negative things? _____

4 Find the words in the box in the report. Then write them in the correct column below.

also	~~and~~	as	because	but	However
~~In conclusion~~	What's more	overall			

Giving more information	Contrasting information	Giving reasons	Giving a conclusion
and			In conclusion

Language focus: *a*, *an* and *the*

5 Complete the sentences with the correct words. Then look at the report to check your answers.

1 I went to visit *a / the* town's new public library this week.
2 It's located in *a / the* new building in the High Street.
3 The library uses all *a / the* latest technology.
4 Members can use *an / the* Internet for free.
5 Borrowing *a / the* book is now computerised.
6 There are some things I preferred about *an / the* old building.
7 *A / The* new library is *a / the* great improvement on the old one.
8 It makes *a / the* town a *a / the* better, more modern place to live in.

UNIT 10 New & Old

Preparing to write

6 Think about a new facility in your town/city or a town/city near you, for example a museum, school, university, hospital, sports centre, cultural centre, etc. Make notes about where it is, what it offers people, and the things you like and don't like about it.

Writing

7 Write a report for other students about the new facility. Organise your report into four paragraphs: an introduction, positive things, negative things and a conclusion. Use the Useful language to help you.

Useful language

- I would like to tell the rest of the class about …
- My impression of the new … was very positive / negative.
- … that's something that the old … didn't have.
- There are some things I preferred about the old …
- I think the new … is a great improvement on the old one.
- It makes the town / city a better, more modern place to live in.

Audioscript

Unit 1

Pronunciation 1

1. My name is Doctor Claudia Wirz, that's W-I-R-Z.
2. My email address is P Ferguson, that's P-F-E-R-G-U-S-O-N at globalnet dot com.
3. I live at thirty-five Apollonos street. I'll spell that for you: A-P-O double L-O-N-O-S.
4. I work for Equinox Consulting. That's spelt E-Q-U-I-N-O-X.
5. I was born in Edinburgh, Scotland. That's E-D-I-N-B-U-R-G-H.
6. The concert takes place in Acacia Park. I'll spell that for you: A-C-A-C-I-A.

Pronunciation 2

1. What do you do here?
2. I take care of the computer system.
3. So I can ask you for help with IT problems.
4. No, you have to call the help desk for that.
5. Oh, what's the number?

Listening

My sister and I are identical twins. That means that we both came from the same egg which split in two in the womb. We have the same genetic make-up and when we were young, we looked exactly the same, even our parents couldn't always tell us apart. We're now in our early thirties and although we still look very similar, our appearance has been affected by our lifestyles.

We do have quite similar personalities, but our tastes and interests are quite different. I love sports and I'm generally more active than my sister, so I'm slimmer than her and her face is slightly more rounded than mine. We dress differently too. She wears more feminine clothes; skirts and dresses, whereas I usually go for trousers or shorts. My hair's quite short and slightly blond because I spend a lot of time outdoors, but my sister's got long, brown hair.

We're very close to each other and we often go on holiday together. People we meet always guess that we're sisters, but the differences are quite obvious, so we don't get mixed up any more.

Unit 2

Listening

According to the World Health Organisation, more than 20% of the world's population, that's more than a billion people, don't have clean, safe drinking water. Unclean water carries diseases and millions of people, many of them young children, die every year from diseases caused by dirty water. Many international organisations are working to improve water purification facilities in some of the world's poorest countries. But, the equipment needed to purify water for a whole community is often very expensive.

One simple solution to the problem of unclean drinking water is a special straw which cleans water as you drink it. The straw is a plastic tube which contains special chemicals. These chemicals remove the harmful bacteria from the water as it passes through. It's very easy to use; you just suck water up through the straw.

Of course, this isn't the answer for everyone and we still need to build more water purification facilities. But it can help to save lives now and it's especially good for people in remote areas or when they're away from their home.

Unit 3

Listening

I work as an art curator for a large art gallery. I look after the gallery's collection of paintings and sculptures. My main job is to make sure that the works of art are kept in the right conditions. The gallery has to be the right temperature, for example. I also keep records of all the works and organise the displays.

As a child I always loved painting pictures. I wasn't a very good artist myself, but I started visiting galleries and I became interested in art. I studied Art History at university. I particularly love Italian art and I spent a year in Italy when I left university. I was working in a restaurant in the evenings and I spent all day visiting museums and galleries. Then I worked for a few years as an art researcher at a museum. I mostly helped to fix old paintings. I really enjoyed working so close to great works of art. Sometimes I used to spend weeks on one painting and I really got to know every little detail.

In my job now, I want to help visitors enjoy the paintings as much as I do. I write the labels which go with them. A good label can really help someone to understand a painting. Many paintings have a story to tell and some background information can bring that story to life.

Audioscript

Unit 4

Listening

A: You're currently working on a new development of eco-houses. What exactly is an eco-house?
B: Well, we're planning to build a group of 20 net-zero carbon homes. A net-zero carbon house is one that, over a year, doesn't use any carbon.
A: But how is that possible?
B: Well, obviously the houses will use energy, for heating and lighting and all the usual things we use electricity for. But because of the design, they'll be very energy efficient and will use much less energy than a traditional home. They'll include technology to reduce energy consumption; special walls and windows which stop heat being lost, for example. But what's more exciting is that the houses will also be able to produce their own electricity using solar panels on the roof. That's how we reach the zero carbon figure, because they'll produce as much energy as they use.
A: That sounds very exciting. So when will these homes be ready for people to live in?
B: Well, we plan to start work on the site next month and we hope to finish the first houses in about 18 months' time.
A: But won't these houses be very expensive with all that special technology? How much are they going to cost?
B: The prices will vary, because this is going to be a mixed development, with some three and four-bedroom family homes and also one and two-bedroom apartments. The prices will be slightly higher than an average home, but the residents will get that money back in a few years because they'll save on their energy bills.

Unit 5

Pronunciation 1

1 Employees can park in front of the office.
2 You can't make personal calls from your desk.
3 You can work flexible hours.
4 You must eat breakfast on the morning of the race.
5 You can't hire surfing equipment at the beach.
6 You mustn't bring a bag with you.

Listening

People around the world spend their leisure time in different ways. The most popular hobbies in different countries are often influenced by lifestyle and the weather.

In the United States, people often work long hours and don't get very much holiday time, so it's not surprising that most people spend their leisure time close to home. The most popular leisure activities listed by Americans are reading, watching TV and spending time with family. Next on the list is gardening. Every weekend, you'll find people out in their back gardens, cutting the grass in the summer or raking leaves in the autumn.

Australia has a warm, dry climate and an outdoor culture. People like to spend most of their free time outside. Most Australians live near to the coast, so going to the beach is like a national hobby. Fishing is a very popular activity, so are surfing and boating. In fact, anything that involves being in or near the water.

Leisure activities in Canada are strongly influenced by the weather. The winters here are long and hard. In some areas, there's snow on the ground for almost six months of the year and average temperatures are below freezing. So it's no surprise that the national sport is ice hockey. People support their local hockey team and over a million Canadians play hockey. These days, fewer people are playing than they used to and golf is actually becoming more popular than ice hockey among Canadians.

Unit 6

Extend your vocabulary 2

A: My computer's stopped working. When I click on the screen, nothing happens.
B: Nothing happens at all?
A: That's right.
B: Have you tried using the keyboard instead?
A: Yep. Still nothing.
B: I think we'll have to shut down and start again.
A: Okay. But won't I lose what I was working on?
B: I'm afraid so. When did you last save your work?
A: Oh, a few minutes ago.
B: Are you sure?
A: Definitely.
B: Then you won't lose too much.

Pronunciation 2

1 www.google.com
2 news.bbc.co.uk
3 en.wikipedia.org
4 j.smith21@hotmail.com
5 h_stein@webmail.ch

Listening

Teachers often tell me that students nowadays are less interested in maths. And it's certainly true that fewer students are studying maths at university level. But why is this? Some people say that we simply don't need to know how to do calculations in our head nowadays. It's much quicker and easier to use the calculator function on your mobile phone. But I'd argue that the problem lies in the way we teach maths at school. The maths we teach just isn't relevant in the modern world. Take fractions, for example. Yes, there are some common fractions that we still use in everyday life, such as a half, a third or a quarter. But why do we need a number like twelve over fifteen, when nought point eight gives the same information so much more directly? Fractions had a place in the past, when people did difficult calculations by hand, but in the digital age, they're simply not relevant to most people. Too much time spent on fractions in maths class is of little practical use and just turns kids off maths. I think we should forget fractions and spend more time on really useful maths like decimals and percentages.

Unit 7

Listening

The first people didn't buy goods from each other with money. They used a barter system, exchanging personal possessions for other goods that they wanted. Animals were often exchanged, and food products too, like fruit and vegetables.

The first metal currency was produced in China about 3,000 years ago. The coins had a hole in the middle so people could put them together to make a chain. In Europe, gold and silver coins first appeared in Turkey and Greece in about 500 B.C. The Romans also used gold and silver coins, and these had great value.

The Chinese were also the first to create banknotes, about 2,000 years ago. These notes were made of thin leather, usually deerskin. The first actual paper currency was used in China from the 9th to the 15th century, many years before it was used in Europe. But the Chinese had problems with inflation.

In 1816 the 'gold standard' was created in England as a solution to the problem of inflation. This linked the national currency, sterling, to a certain amount of gold. But the gold standard was the cause of the economic problems in the 1930s and many countries decided that the government and banks would try to control inflation and not to link currency directly to gold.

Today electronic money, or digital cash, is exchanged over the internet, and this virtual money looks like it will be with us to stay.

Unit 8

Pronunciation 2

1 If I could live anywhere in the world, I'd have an apartment in Paris.
2 If you could change one thing about your house, what would you change?
3 If we have children, we'll probably move to a bigger place.
4 We'll have to hire a van if we move again.
5 I'd keep lots of pets if we lived in the country

Listening

Dacha season

This week is the start of the dacha season when thousands of Russians leave the city in search of some fresh country air. Many families in Russia and other former Soviet countries have dachas, or holiday homes in the country. People living in cities go out to their dacha at weekends, especially during the summer, to relax and enjoy the countryside. It's a cheap way to take a break from city life. Around 60% of people in Moscow leave the Russian capital to spend their weekends out of town in the summer. And for city dwellers, who often live in large apartment blocks, dachas also have gardens where they grow their own fruit and vegetables.

Traditionally, a dacha is a simple house often on only one floor. Many dachas are made of wood and have little heating or hot water, so they aren't usually occupied during the cold Russian winter. The dacha season usually starts with the first of May holiday when many Russians go to their dacha to start planting fruit and vegetables. With another public holiday on the ninth of May, many people take off the time in-between to enjoy nearly two weeks at their dacha, away from the stress and pollution of city life.

Unit 9

Listening

A: So, how much exercise should we be doing to keep fit?
B: Well, most medical experts say that you ought to do around 30 minutes of exercise five times a week. But some research shows that 30 minutes of exercise, such as walking, three times a week still has some health benefits.
A: And is walking okay or do we need to do something more energetic?
B: Of course, what exercise is best for you depends on how old you are and how healthy you are. Some experts say that ideally you should include some exercise that raises your heart rate and makes you out of breath, such as running.
A: And what are the benefits of regular exercise?
B: Most people know that if you exercise regularly, you can reduce the risk of many illnesses such as heart disease. You'll also have more energy. Many offices now have gyms because employees who exercise at work are happier and more productive. Exercise could even help you live longer. According to a recent study, men in their fifties who exercise at least three times a week live 2.3 years longer than those men who do no exercise at all.

Audioscript

Unit 10

Pronunciation 1

1. a side street
2. the railway station
3. the market place
4. public transport
5. a bus stop
6. playing games
7. the railway tracks
8. straight away
9. a college student
10. air travel

Listening

Archaeologists believe that the oldest city in the world is Damascus, in Syria. Research shows that people were living there more than 10,000 years ago. The ancient city is now a UNESCO World Heritage site.

The world's oldest working clock is in Salisbury Cathedral in England. The clock was made in 1386, so it has been ticking for more than 600 years. Although a mechanical clock was already working in Milan, Italy by 1335, the Salisbury clock is the oldest known to still be working today.

A Buddhist holy text known as the Diamond Sutra is thought to be the oldest surviving printed book. It was made in 868 AD, making it more than a thousand years old. It was found in north-west China in 1907 and consists of a scroll of grey paper with Chinese characters, wrapped around a wooden pole.

Two institutions lay claim to the title of the oldest university. The University of Al-Karaouine in Fez, Morocco, and Al-Azhar University in Cairo, Egypt, are both more than a thousand years old. The oldest European university is in Bologna, Italy. It was founded in 1088 and was the first to use the word university to describe a place of learning.

Answer Key

Unit 1

Grammar 1A
1 do	5 Are
2 does	6 did
3 is	7 do
4 Do	8 Do

Grammar 1B
1 Are	5 Do
2 Do	6 does
3 are	7 did
4 do	

Grammar 2
1 What	5 What
2 How	6 How
3 What	7 How
4 How	

Grammar 3
1 hate	5 get	9 sells
2 send	6 give	10 are
3 put	7 order	11 has
4 do	8 adds	12 doesn't want

Grammar 4
1 I always take my keys with me when I go out.
2 I usually carry my wallet with me.
3 I often pay for things by credit card, but I always have some cash in my wallet for small things.
4 My mobile phone is almost always in my pocket.
5 I go to the gym every morning so my bag is usually full of my sports clothes.
6 I hardly ever take a bag with me; I usually just put things in my pockets.

Grammar 5
1 Correct	5 Correct
2 Correct	6 Incorrect
3 Incorrect	7 Incorrect
4 Correct	8 Incorrect

Vocabulary 1A

Hair	Height	Weight	Age
bald	tall	fat	old
curly	short	slim	young
straight	medium-height	overweight	middle-aged

Vocabulary 1B
1 a	5 b
2 d	6 b
3 d	7 c
4 a	8 c

Extend your vocabulary 1
1 looks like	4 look like
2 looks, looks like	5 looks
3 looks, look like	6 looks like

Vocabulary 2A

Friends	Family
classmate	wife
acquaintance	husband
colleague	brother
neighbour	sister

Vocabulary 2B
1 classmates	4 colleague
2 wife	5 friend
3 acquaintance	6 neighbour

Extend your vocabulary 2
1 in	4 keep
2 lost	5 out of
3 with	6 get

Extend your vocabulary 3
1 takes place
2 taken part
3 in place of her
4 all over the place
5 out of place
6 in the first place
7 my place

Pronunciation 1
1 Wirz	4 Equinox
2 pferguson	5 Edinburgh
3 Apollonos	6 Acacia

Pronunciation 2
1 a	4 c
2 b	5 b
3 a	

Listening
1 b	4 a
2 a	5 a
3 b	6 b

Reading
1
The student's own answers
2
1 For work, for education, for a better life
2 Parents have to find new friends, children have to change schools, grandparents live far from their grandchildren
3
1 true
2 false
3 false
4
1 generation	3 urbanisation
2 population	4 rural communities

5
1 have	5 have
2 are getting	6 are
3 is	7 doesn't have
4 live	8 are growing

Writing
2
Full name, position/job title, name for friends, country of birth, education, work history, languages, interests/free time activities, job description, family
3
1 both	4 too
2 and	5 so
3 but	6 also

Answer Key

Unit 2

Grammar 1A

countable	countable or uncountable	uncountable
nut	steak	pasta
sandwich	chocolate	soup
potato	coffee	bread
		meat

Grammar 1B
1 a   4 some   7 any
2 some   5 some   8 a
3 –   6 a   9 –

Grammar 2A
1 much   5 much
2 many   6 many
3 many   7 much
4 many   8 many

Grammar 2B
1 a few   4 a little, too many
2 enough   5 many
3 A lot of, much

Grammar 3
1 to cook, to have   4 to find
2 to make   5 sell
3 to use, go   6 to visit, get

Grammar 4
1 Before you start cooking, check the recipe **to** make sure you have all the ingredients.
2 You will need an onion, some garlic, some beef and a tin of tomatoes **to** make a basic pasta sauce.
3 Put some oil in a frying pan **to** cook while you cut the onions and garlic.
4 Fry the onions and garlic gently. Be careful, it's easy **to** burn them.
5 Add the meat to the pan. Keep stirring everything **to** stop it from sticking.
6 Pour in the tomatoes and stir well **to** mix.
7 Cover the pan and leave it **to** cook gently for 45 minutes.

Vocabulary 1A
1 c   2 d   3 b   4 a

Vocabulary 1B
1 breakfast   4 snack
2 lunch   5 dinner
3 eat   6 serve

Extend your vocabulary
1 taste like   4 bitter taste
2 tastes awful   5 tastes of
3 taste sweet

Vocabulary 2A
1 fork   4 frying pan
2 knife   5 saucepan
3 spoon   6 plate

Vocabulary 2B
1 c   2 e   3 f   4 a   5 d   6 b

Vocabulary 3A
1 mug   3 glass   5 cup
2 bottle   4 carton

Vocabulary 3B
1 two coffees   4 any orange juice
2 some milk   5 a few glasses
3 tea, any milk   6 the tap water

Vocabulary 4
Across
2 eyes   5 fingers   7 feet   8 brain
Down
1 heart   3 skin   4 knee   6 ears

Pronunciation 1

/k/	/tʃ/
carton	cheese
cup	chewing gum
cake	chop
snack	match
breakfast	
ice cubes	

Pronunciation 2

	/tə/	/tuː/
1		✔
2	✔	
3		✔
4	✔	
5		✔
6		✔
7	✔	

Listening
1 True
2 True
3 False – The speaker says 'Many international organisations are working to improve water purification facilities in some of the world's poorest countries,' so these facilities exist.
4 True
5 True
6 False – The speaker says about the straws that 'this isn't the answer for everyone.'

Reading
1
The student's own answers
2
1 a lot of   2 a lot of   3 don't eat
3
1 J, LA   4 M, LA
2 J, F   5 F
3 M, LA   6 J
4
1 You need time and clear information.
2 Because experts change their advice about what food is good and bad for you.
3 Not many. / (Only) a few.
4 It looks good and portions are small.
5 Because the French live long, healthy lives, but they eat some things that are not healthy.
6 It's not just the ingredients that are important, but about how we eat.
5
1 no time   4 To help
2 too much   5 to know
3 a few   6 don't / enough

Writing
2

food adjectives	food nouns
simple	ingredients
healthy	*menu*
delicious	soup
fresh	sandwich
tasty	tea
local	coffee
vegetarian	cake
typical	chocolate
original	fish
exciting	meat
special	dish
	vegetables
	recipe
	taste
	curry
	noodles
	rice
	chicken

3
The student's own answers
4
The student's own answers
5
The student's own answers

Answer Key

Unit 3

Grammar 1A
1 watched
2 played
3 studied
4 visited
5 dropped, smashed
6 pressed, stopped
7 planned, arrived

Grammar 1B
1 paid
2 wrote
3 left, went
4 shot
5 won
6 stole
7 found

Grammar 2
1 began
2 was studying
3 finished
4 had
5 taught
6 was working
7 wrote
8 worked
9 came
10 was sitting
11 completed
12 was living

Grammar 3A
1 used to listen
2 didn't use to like
3 used to go
4 used to be
5 used to complain
6 did you use to like

Grammar 3B
1 Before television, people used to listen to the radio for news.
2 People used to go to the cinema to watch news films.
3 In the early days of TV, there didn't use to be programmes all day.
4 Families used to sit together around the TV in the evening.
5 When I was young, we used to have a black and white TV.
6 And there didn't use to be as many different TV channels as there are today.
7 I can remember when we used to record programmes onto video cassettes.
8 What programmes did you use to enjoy as a child?

Grammar 4
1 Past
2 Present
3 Past
4 Past
5 Present
6 Past
7 Past
8 Past
9 Present
10 Present
11 Present

Vocabulary 1
1 d 2 a 3 e 4 c 5 b

Extend your vocabulary 1
1 discovered
2 discovers
3 discoveries
4 undiscovered
5 discovery

Vocabulary 2
1 armchair
2 sofa
3 lamp
4 mirror
5 shelf
6 curtain

Extend your vocabulary 2
1 Correct
2 Incorrect
3 Correct
4 Correct
5 Incorrect
6 Correct

Vocabulary 3
1 orchestra, musicians
2 group, singer
3 concert, audience
4 drummer, guitarist

Vocabulary 4
1 player
2 earphones
3 press
4 button
5 record
6 cassette
7 rewind
8 forward

Vocabulary 5A

Positive ☺	Negative ☹
excited	angry
happy	bored
relaxed	sad
cheerful	miserable
calm	scared
	anxious
	tense

Vocabulary 5B
1 miserable
2 cheerful
3 excited
4 anxious
5 scared
6 bored
7 angry
8 tense
9 relaxed

Vocabulary 6
1 d 2 c 3 a 4 f 5 b 6 e

Pronunciation 1

/t/ or /d/	/ɪd/
walked	decided
stopped	hated
looked	needed
worked	started
opened	wanted
listened	
asked	

Pronunciation 2
1 My family used to live in Africa.
2 I used to walk miles to school.
3 We didn't use to have electricity.
4 My mother used to collect water from the river.
5 She used to sing while she worked.

Listening
1 He enjoyed painting pictures when he was young.
2 He became interested in art.
3 He studied Art History at university.
4 He spent a year in Italy.
5 He worked as an art researcher.
6 He works as an art curator at a large gallery.

Reading
1
1 A music project which offers free musical instruments and tuition.
2 Venezuela
3 For poor children
2
1 seventies
2 social
3 musical
4 youth
5 similar
3
1 tuition
2 violence
3 district
4 inequalities
5 elsewhere
4
1 began
2 found
3 didn't (just) take
4 tried
5 set
6 was
7 saw
8 wanted

Writing
1
The student's own answers
2
1 ✔ 2 ✔ 3 ✔ 4 ✔ 5 ✔ 6 ✗
3
1 sad
2 clever
3 unhappy
4 exciting
5 popular
6 successful
4
Group 1: author, writer
Group 2: book, novel
Group 3: plot, story, tale
Group 4: popular, well-loved

Answer Key

Unit 4

Grammar 1A
1 correct
2 incorrect – Use the infinitive with *to* (*to work*) after *want*.
3 incorrect – Use the infinitive with *to* (*to do*) after *would like*.
4 correct
5 correct
6 incorrect – Use a verb with *-ing* (*finding*) after *look forward to*.
7 incorrect – Use *I'd like* + the infinitive with *to* (*to have*) to talk about future hopes or plans.
8 correct

Grammar 1B
1 plans to open   4 like to live
2 going to apply 5 want to experience
3 hope to get   6 looking forward to going

Grammar 2
1 Are you going to 5 I'm going to get
2 I'm doing   6 I'm driving
3 are you staying   7 Are you going to stay
4 are you getting   8 I'm going to come

Grammar 3
1 will get
2 will be able to access
3 will be
4 won't need
5 won't use
6 will be able to talk
7 will be able to translate
8 will improve
9 won't be able to steal

Grammar 4
1 you arrive   5 you get   9 you make
2 you'll meet 6 he'll tell 10 you'll lose
3 He'll go   7 You'll be 11 will tell
4 you start   8 will ask   12 you get

Grammar 5A
1 f   2 c   3 e   4 a   5 b   6 g   7 d

Grammar 5B
A: Where **are** you going on holiday this year?
B: We plan **to** go to the coast. We'd like **to** stay near the beach. So the boys will **be** able to go surfing.
A: Are you going **to** stay in a hotel?
B: No, **we'll** probably rent a cottage.

Vocabulary 1A
1 wonderful   4 tense
2 excellent   5 miserable
3 happy

Vocabulary 1B
1 wonderful   4 good-looking, intelligent
2 bad   5 clever
3 well-off, beautiful

Vocabulary 2A

natural disasters	environmental issues	social issues
earthquakes floods	pollution climate change carbon emissions	poverty homelessness crime

Vocabulary 2B
1 aid   5 environmental
2 natural   6 climate
3 earthquakes 7 emissions
4 war   8 efficient

Vocabulary 3
1 back   3 away
2 around   4 up, together

Vocabulary 4
1 become   4 arrive   7 receive
2 receive 5 become   8 receive
3 become   6 arrive

Vocabulary 5
1 lake   3 desert   5 forest
2 river   4 mountains 6 ocean

Extend your vocabulary
1 worried   4 interested 7 tired
2 bored   5 terrifying 8 amazing
3 surprising 6 frightened

Pronunciation 1

oO	Oo	Ooo	oOo
disease	hunger footprint issue	poverty energy	recycle efficient pollution

Pronunciation 2
1 /red/   4 /teə(r)z/   7 /lɪvz/
2 /riːd/   5 /kləʊz/   8 /laɪvz/
3 /tɪə(r)z/ 6 /kləʊs/

Listening
1 c   2 b   3 a   4 c   5 a

Reading
1
1 8   4 Japan
2 2050   5 social, economic
3 Uganda

2
1 People are living longer and families are having fewer children.
2 People of working age will have to pay more in taxes to pay for pensions and we will need more healthcare workers and fewer teachers.
3 The student's own answer

3
1 ageing   3 trend
2 older   4 retire

4
The 'grey pound' is money that the elderly spend.

5
1 will work   4 will be
2 won't retire 5 will use
3 will employ 6 won't be

Writing
1
Max and Damien are work colleagues.

2
I'm (=I am) just writing to check your travel plans for your visit next week.
What time's (=time is) your flight due to arrive? The airport is just outside the city, so it's (it is) probably best to get a taxi to the office. It should cost about €30. Have you got the address?
When you get to the office, I'll (= I will) introduce you to everyone and go through the schedule for the week. Then I'll (= I will) take you to your hotel. In the evening, we'll (= we will) all go out for a meal.

3
The language of the email is quite formal.
1 Dear Damien
2 Thanks for your email.
3 I'm afraid I don't know the address.
4 I look forward to meeting you on Monday.
5 Best wishes.

4
1 e   2 c   3 a   4 f   5 b   6 d

5 –

6
1 My train is due **to** arrive at 16.30.
2 I'll **get** a bus to the city centre.
3 I plan **to** drive to the conference centre.
4 I'll call you when **I get** to the airport.
5 Someone **will meet** you at the station.
6 If **it's** raining, I'll get a taxi.

Answer Key

Unit 5

Grammar 1A
1 has 5 work
2 worked 6 have
3 got 7 has
4 have 8 speak

Grammar 1B
1 incorrect – *many banks (they)* + *have*
2 correct
3 incorrect – you cannot contract *have to* as a modal verb
4 incorrect – we use *have to* as a modal verb, not *have got to*
5 incorrect – the negative of *have* as a main verb is *don't have*
6 correct
7 correct
8 incorrect – the negative of the modal *have to* is *don't have to*

Grammar 2A
1 b 2 d 3 a 4 c 5 e

Grammar 2B
1 don't have to buy
2 can run, don't have to sign
3 can always train
4 have to do
5 must wear
6 mustn't go

Grammar 3A
1 jogging 4 cooking
2 skiing 5 swimming
3 cycling 6 snowboarding

Grammar 3B
1 working 4 doing 7 stand
2 enjoy 5 mind 8 Writing
3 sitting 6 learning

Grammar 4A
1 been 4 driven 7 spoken
2 delivered 5 had 8 written
3 chosen 6 met

Grammar 4B
1 been 4 been
2 gone 5 been
3 gone 6 gone

Grammar 5
1 Have you ever done 6 I've never worked
2 I've had 7 I've done
3 I worked 8 I left
4 I picked 9 I put
5 It was

Grammar 6
1 Have you ever skied before?
2 I've only tried a few times on lower slopes.
3 I've never been on a ski lift.
4 Cycling is good for you.
5 I enjoy riding in the countryside.
6 I don't cycle in the city without wearing a helmet.
7 Can anyone go surfing?
8 You have to be quite fit.
9 You must be a good swimmer.

Vocabulary 1
Across
5 lawyer 6 politician 7 teacher
Down
1 journalist 2 waiter 3 builder
4 doctor

Vocabulary 2
1 Workers 5 breaks
2 hours 6 security
3 shifts 7 training
4 wages 8 employ

Extend your vocabulary
1 work, jobs 4 jobs
2 job 5 work, jobs
3 work

Vocabulary 3
1 in, on 3 down
2 off 4 to, in

Vocabulary 4
1 c 2 g 3 a 4 h 5 d 6 e 7 b 8 f

Pronunciation 1
1 can 4 must
2 can't 5 can't
3 can 6 mustn't

Pronunciation 2
1 Many <u>young</u> people spend their <u>evenings</u> on social <u>networking</u> websites.
2 <u>Fishing</u> is the most popular hobby in <u>England</u>.
3 On holiday, a lot of people like <u>sitting</u> on the beach, <u>reading</u> a book or just <u>doing nothing</u>.
4 Some people enjoy <u>collecting</u> <u>things</u>, such as stamps or coins.
5 <u>Surfing</u> and <u>skiing</u> are popular sports with <u>young</u> people.

Pronunciation 3
1 got 4 eaten
2 gone 5 paid
3 learnt

Listening

	USA	Australia	Canada
1	✔		
2		✔	
3			✔
4		✔	
5	✔		
6			✔
7			✔
8		✔	

Reading
1
Teleworking means working from home with the help of new technology.
Hot desking is a way of working in which employees don't have their own desk in the office, but use any desk that's available when they come in.

2
1 more easily work from home. ✔
  stay in contact with work when they are not in the office. ✔
2 always work at the same desk. ✔
  stay in the office all day. ✔

3
1 out of the office
2 nine to five
3 keep in touch

4 & 5
1 has, AUX 4 have, MV
2 have, MOD 5 have, MOD
3 has, AUX 6 have, MV

Writing
1
The student's own answers

2
1 don't have to have 3 must be
2 must be 4 must be

3
1 present perfect to talk about past experiences
2 past simple to talk about a specific time in the past
3 past simple to talk about a specific time in the past

4
1 studied 4 taught
2 wrote 5 've taken
3 've worked 6 've never worked

Answer Key

Unit 6

Grammar 1A
1 heavier
2 more slowly
3 faster
4 thinner
5 longer
6 taller
7 more sensitive
8 healthier

Grammar 1B
1 faster
2 taller
3 worse
4 more expensive
5 wetter
6 drier
7 larger
8 bigger
9 more popular

Grammar 1C
1 more quickly, more efficiently
2 more easily
3 better
4 faster
5 worse

Grammar 2
1 My grandparents' lifestyle was much simpler than ours.
2 They worked just as hard as we do.
3 Things happened much more slowly in those days.
4 So people's lifestyles weren't as stressful as ours.
5 They were probably a bit fitter than people nowadays.
6 They had to walk much further than we do.
7 But they weren't as healthy as we are.
8 People were much more likely to die of common diseases.

Grammar 3
1 the loudest
2 the most dangerous
3 the most popular
4 the heaviest
5 the coldest
6 the largest
7 The deepest
8 the driest

Grammar 4
These phrases are incorrect:
3 switch off it
4 print out them
7 take out it
8 charge up it

Vocabulary 1A
1 c 2 h 3 e 4 g 5 f 6 b 7 a 8 d

Vocabulary 1B
1 popular
2 cheaper
3 wider
4 stressful
5 nervous
6 safer
7 satisfied
8 easier

Extend your vocabulary 1
1 spirits
2 down
3 heart
4 top
5 air

Vocabulary 2
1 scholarship
2 scientist
3 teacher
4 researcher
5 weakness
6 economist
7 relationship

Extend your vocabulary 2
1 That's right
2 Yep
3 Ok
4 I'm afraid so
5 Definitely

Vocabulary 3
1 laptop
2 keyboard
3 computer screen
4 headphones
5 mobile phone
6 text message

Vocabulary 4A
1 c 2 a 3 e 4 g 5 d 6 h 7 b 8 f

Vocabulary 4B
1 up
2 in
3 out
4 down
5 down, off
6 in
7 on
8 down

Vocabulary 5
1 So was
2 So did
3 Neither has
4 So does
5 too
6 Neither do

Pronunciation 1
1 engineer
2 far
3 portable
4 research
5 spa

Pronunciation 2
1 www.google.com
2 news.bbc.co.uk
3 en.wikipedia.org
4 j.smith21@hotmail.com
5 h_stein@webmail.ch

Listening
1 less interested
2 Fewer
3 calculation
4 common
5 useful
6 relevant
7 less

Reading
1
1 miniseries
2 microchips
3 minivan
4 microwave

2
A minicomputer is the largest; a personal computer (PC) is the smallest.

3
1 a 2 b 3 c 4 b 5 a

4
1 portable
2 affordable
3 available

5
1 acceptable 3 noticeable
2 avoidable   4 recyclable

6
1 so has
2 plug your computer into
3 most popular
4 as well as
5 neither do
6 much cheaper

Writing
1
1 Advantages
2 Disadvantages
3 Advantages
4 Disadvantages

2
1 The most annoying
2 better
3 more convenient
4 easier
5 the worst
6 more polite
7 safer
8 the most useful

3
These things would be suitable for an introduction:
background to the topic – *mobile phones have become more common across the world*
general questions – *Are mobile phones bad for society?*
the topic of the essay – *mobile phones have both advantages and disadvantages*

4
The student's own answers

Answer Key

Unit 7

Grammar 1A

for	since
several hours	last Friday
two weeks	1956
20 years	5th June
a few minutes	4 o'clock
a long time	the 10th century

Grammar 1B

1 since 5 since
2 since 6 for
3 for   7 since
4 in   8 in

Grammar 2

1 People have (**already**) travelled into space (**already**).
2 Men haven't (**yet**) been to other planets (**yet**).
3 Have spacecraft landed on Mars (**yet**)?
4 Many European countries have (**already**) adopted the Euro (**already**).
5 Has Britain started using the Euro (**yet**)?
6 Scientists have (**already**) discovered cures for many diseases (**already**).
7 Doctors have (**already**) managed to transplant all kinds of organs (**already**).
8 We haven't (**yet**) found a cure for the common cold (**yet**).

Grammar 3

1 a 2 b 3 a 4 a 5 a 6 b

Vocabulary 1

1 In   5 in
2 at   6 at
3 on   7 in
4 On

Vocabulary 2

Across
3 February 4 seasons 7 July
8 spring   9 morning
Down
1 Wednesday 2 January
5 evening   6 second 8 summer

Vocabulary 3

1 overtime 4 save
2 zones   5 waste
3 spend   6 free

Vocabulary 4

1 c 2 e 3 a 4 f 5 d 6 b

Vocabulary 5

1 take 5 spend
2 pay   6 earn
3 earn 7 take
4 owe   8 pay

Extend your vocabulary

1 lend   5 borrow
2 borrow 6 lent
3 lend   7 borrowed
4 borrow

Pronunciation 1

	/aɪ/	/eɪ/	a different sound
1	✔		
2		✔	
3		✔	
4			✔
5	✔		
6			✔

Pronunciation 2

1 mortgage 4 house
2 buy   5 both
3 home   6 alone

Listening

1
1 d 2 a 3 f 4 b 5 g 6 e 7 c
2
1 hole   4 the 1930s
2 leather 5 inflation
3 before

Reading

1
Suggested answer: A society in which people don't use cash to pay for the things that they buy.
2
1 Cash is the most popular way to pay for small purchases.
2 More than half.
3 You touch your mobile phone to a reader and the payment is made instantly.
4 South Korea.
5 It would take a long time for everyone to change their mobile phones.
3
1 cash   5 PIN
2 credit card 6 purchase
3 debit card   7 transaction
4 coins
4
1 out 4 over, around
2 for 5 in
3 by

Writing

1
1 b 2 c 3 e 4 d 5 f 6 a
2
Suggested answers:
Most people travel from New York to London by plane these days, and many homes have a dishwasher and electric lights. New inventions include the plane, the dishwasher and the light bulb.
3
Suggested answer: People watch television, use the internet and their computer, read newspapers and go to the cinema.
4
The student's own answer
5
1 It is certainly true that **we / people** have a lot more free time than our grandparents did.
2 I think **it** that people could use their free time more wisely.
3 I believe that **it** is important for families to spend time together.
4 We should spend more of our free time **for** doing exercise and outdoor activities.
5 I don't think that **there** are enough things for young people to do in their free time.

Answer Key

Unit 8

Grammar 1A
1 is known
2 is located
3 is officially recognised
4 was originally called
5 was changed
6 was connected
7 was constructed
8 was built
9 was created
10 was printed

Grammar 1B
1 was designed   5 are visited
2 was built   6 were used
3 was finished   7 were taken
4 is used   8 aren't allowed

Grammar 2
1 will pay   5 can call
2 you are   6 you take part
3 lose   7 you pay
4 is delayed   8 you can visit

Grammar 3A
1 d   2 c   3 f   4 b   5 e   6 a

Grammar 3B
1 were   5 wouldn't stop
2 'd paint   6 didn't speak
3 knew   7 'd live
4 found   8 'd grow

Grammar 4
1 b   2 a   3 b   4 b   5 b   6 a

Vocabulary 1
1 kitchen   4 dining room
2 bathroom   5 living room
3 bedroom   6 hall

Extend your vocabulary 1
1 home   5 home
2 homework   6 home
3 house   7 home
4 house   8 housework

Vocabulary 2
1 out of   7 across
2 along   8 down
3 past   9 through
4 into   10 into
5 across   11 up
6 around

Extend your vocabulary 2
1 drive   4 ride
2 tour   5 trips
3 trip   6 journey, flight, ride

Vocabulary 3A
Across
4 rabbit   5 budgie   8 dog   10 snake
Down
1 horse   2 spider   3 mouse
6 goldfish 7 hamster 9 cat

Vocabulary 3B
1 kept, pet   4 tail
2 legs   5 owners
3 fur, ears   6 domestic

Vocabulary 4
1 at   4 about
2 of   5 of
3 in   6 of

Vocabulary 5
1 Tourism   5 tourist attraction
2 visited   6 tourist activities
3 on holiday   7 tourists
4 travellers   8 souvenirs

Pronunciation 1
1 hour   4 flight
2 kitchen   5 phone
3 ghost   6 fish

Pronunciation 2
1 I could live, I'd have
2 could change, would you change
3 have, we'll probably move
4 We'll have to, move
5 I'd keep, lived

Listening
1 c   2 b   3 a   4 c   5 b

Reading
1
Nomads are people who do not have a fixed home and move from place to place, often following the animals which they herd or hunt.
The article mentions Mongolian, Sámi and Bedouin nomads.

2

	Mongolians	the Sámi	the Bedouin
1	✔	✔	✔
2		✔	✔
3	✔		
4		✔	✔
5	✔		✔
6		✔	

3
1 are made   5 is threatened
2 is covered   6 is legally protected
3 are packed   7 can only be done
4 are rebuilt   8 are divided

4
don't move, won't find

Writing
1
Text 1 was written by a visitor. Text 2 is from a guidebook.

2
1 c   2 a   3 g   4 b   5 f   6 d   7 e

3
1 sightseeing   5 landmark
2 explore   6 tourist attraction
3 atmosphere   7 stroll
4 buzzing

Answer Key

Unit 9

Grammar 1A
1 incorrect – Use *shouldn't* + infinitive (*go out* – NOT *going*)
2 correct
3 incorrect – Use *ought to* + infinitive (*eat*)
4 incorrect – Use *mustn't* + infinitive (*go* – NOT *to go*)
5 correct
6 correct
7 incorrect – Use *must* + infinitive (*read* – NOT *to read*)

Grammar 1B
1 should get up
2 should drink
3 shouldn't drink
4 must take
5 ought to take
6 shouldn't wear
7 should choose
8 ought to try

Grammar 2
1 couldn't keep
2 had to be used
3 could keep
4 didn't have to eat
5 could store
6 had to cook

Grammar 3A
1 'd injured
2 'd hurt
3 'd tripped
4 'd eaten
5 had broken
6 'd taken
7 'd already promised
8 had crashed

Grammar 3B
1 he'd injured his leg
2 Michael had hurt his knee
3 he'd eaten some bad food
4 it had broken down
5 Theo had promised to take his girlfriend away
6 his computer had crashed

Grammar 4
1 the team had played
2 she'd trained / she had trained, she was / was
3 he was, they hadn't won / they had not won
4 wasn't playing / was not playing, he'd injured / he had injured
5 it definitely hadn't been / it definitely had not been

Vocabulary 1
1 the matter
2 caught
3 sore
4 blocked
5 well
6 wrong
7 I've got
8 I feel

Vocabulary 2
1 break
2 have
3 stay
4 visit
5 go
6 take
7 cause
8 consult

Vocabulary 3
1 c 2 e 3 a 4 d 5 f 6 b

Vocabulary 4
1 go
2 go
3 play
4 do
5 go
6 do
7 play
8 play
9 play
10 do

Vocabulary 5
1 team
2 players
3 individual
4 winner
5 race
6 losers
7 play
8 go
9 do

Extend your vocabulary
1 won, beat
2 beat
3 was won
4 won, winning
5 won, beating

Vocabulary 6
1 ask, say
2 tells
3 ask
4 asked, told
5 say

Pronunciation 1
1 Different
2 Same
3 Different
4 Same
5 Different
6 Same

Pronunciation 2
1 injection
2 ambulance
3 medicine
4 disease
5 individual

Listening
1 thirty
2 health
3 running
4 regularly
5 happier
6 do

Reading
1
1 Christiaan Barnard
2 1967
3 South Africa
4 Nine hours
5 Eighteen days

2
c

3
1 MT 2 P 3 MT 4 P 5 P 6 P 7 MC

4
1 Operations on animals. Past perfect = *had spent*
2 The woman died. Past perfect = *had died*
3 Surgeons gave up. Past perfect = *had given up*

5
1 had already performed
2 'd developed
3 'd had
4 'd received

Writing
2
1 Make sure
2 You don't need to buy
3 You should get
4 try asking
5 you ought to do
6 You must get
7 It's worth spending
8 Don't be afraid to
9 You could just have

3
Suggested answers

Skiing	Tennis	Cycling	Golf
skis	tennis racket	cycling shorts	golf shoes
ski boots	tennis balls	helmet	golf clubs
ski poles	trainers	bike	golf balls
ski pants	shorts	gloves	golf bag
jacket	t-shirt		
gloves			

Answer Key

Unit 10

Grammar 1A
1 who   6 that
2 which   7 which
3 that   8 who
4 who   9 which
5 which   10 who

Grammar 1B
1 who has recently started
2 who has just been
3 which was first visited
4 which you make
5 which is old
6 who has been doing
7 which many people think is

Grammar 2A
1 b 2 a 3 d 4 c 5 c 6 a 7 d 8 b

Grammar 2B
1 a   6 -   11 the
2 the   7 the   12 the
3 a   8 the   13 the
4 the   9 The
5 The   10 the

Grammar 3
1 d 2 h 3 a 4 e 5 c 6 g 7 b 8 f

Grammar 4
1 both cities   6 both are
2 Both cities have   7 both places
3 Both places are   8 both have
4 neither of them   9 both cities are
5 Both of them are   10 Neither city is

Vocabulary 1
1 mouse   4 blog
2 brunch   5 virus
3 carbon   6 email

Vocabulary 2A
1 f 2 c 3 a 4 g 5 b 6 e 7 d

Vocabulary 2B
1 state   4 country
2 city   5 village
3 capital 6 birthplace

Extend your vocabulary 1
1 cutting-edge   3 innovative
2 latest   4 modern
3 brand   5 fresh

Vocabulary 3A
1 bus   4 motorbike/motorcycle
2 underground   5 taxi
3 bicycle/bike   6 plane/airplane/aeroplane

Vocabulary 3B
1 b 2 b 3 c 4 a 5 c 6 c

Vocabulary 4
1 getting on   5 get on
2 rode   6 get in
3 by bicycle   7 get out
4 driving

Extend your vocabulary 2
1 manufacture   4 developing
2 produced   5 causing
3 designed   6 built

Vocabulary 5
1 player   6 square
2 counter   7 land on
3 board   8 win
4 turn   9 piece
5 roll the dice

Pronunciation 1

	/pl/	/tr/	/st/	/str/
1				✓
2			✓	
3	✓			
4		✓		
5			✓	
6	✓			
7		✓		
8				✓
9			✓	
10		✓		

Pronunciation 2
1 a 2 a 3 b 4 b 5 a

Listening
1
1 city   2 clock   3 text   4 university
2
1 10,000 years   4 printed book
2 working clock   5 1,000 years +
3 England   6 Egypt/Morocco

Reading
1
The student's own answers
2
See answers to 3 below.
3
1 c 2 e 3 f 4 a 5 d 6 b
4
1 The word *encyclopedia* comes from a Greek **phrase**.
2 **No** copies of the *Disciplinae* exist today.
3 The first encyclopedias were **textbooks** for students.
4 Information on the first digital encyclopedias was organized **by subject**.
5 The first encyclopedia on CD-ROM **had audio and video material**.
6 *Wikipedia* is the world's biggest encyclopedia.
5
1 which / that, source
2 which / that, general knowledge
3 who / that, historian
4 who / that, father
5 which / that, volume
6 which / that, key words
6 all answers are in paragraphs 1–3
1 (we) look
2 (printed encyclopedias) were
3 (The Internet) has revolutionised
4 (it) was first used
5 (Aristotle) is sometimes called
6 (The Internet has revolutionised the way) that we look for information.
7 (it was first used) to describe

Writing
1
It's about a library. The missing word is 'library'.
2
It doesn't mention 'How to become a member' but it mentions all the other things.
3
1 D 2 B 3 A 4 C
4

Giving more information	Contrasting information	Giving reasons	Giving a conclusion
and	but	as	*In conclusion*,
also	However,	because	overall
What's more,			

5
1 the   5 a
2 a   6 the
3 the   7 a
4 the   8 the, a

Macmillan Education
4 Crinan Street
London N1 9XW
A division of Springer Nature Limited

Companies and representatives throughout the world

ISBN 978-1-380-03609-4
Pack ISBN 978-1-380-04068-8

Text, design and illustration © Springer Nature Limited 2011
Written by Julie Moore
Additional material by Rob Metcalf

The authors have asserted their right to be identified as the authors of this work in accordance with the Copyright, Designs and Patents Act 1988.

This edition published 2019
First edition entitled "Global" published 2010 by Springer Nature Limited

All rights reserved; no part of this publication may be reproduced, stored in a retrieval system, or transmitted in any form, or by any means, electronic, mechanical, photocopying, recording, or otherwise, without the prior written permission of the publishers.

Designed by eMC Design Limited
Cover design by Springer Nature Ltd
Cover photos: Getty Images/Stockphoto/IgorKovalchuk; Shutterstock/Davydenko Yuliia

The authors and publishers would like to thank the following for permission to reproduce their photographs:

Apple Inc; Bananastock; Brand X; Comstock; Corbis; Creatas; Digital Stock; Digital Vision; Fancy; Getty; Goodshoot; Grapheast; Image 100; Image Source; iStock; Macmillan Publishers Ltd; Medio Images; Pathfinder; Photoalto; Photodisc; Stockbyte

These materials may contain links for third party websites. We have no control over, and are not responsible for, the contents of such third party websites. Please use care when accessing them.

The inclusion of any specific companies, commercial products, trade names or otherwise does not constitute or imply its endorsement or recommendation by Springer Nature Limited.

Printed and bound in Singapore
2022 2021 2020 2019
5 4 3 2 1